Molded for the MIRACULOUS

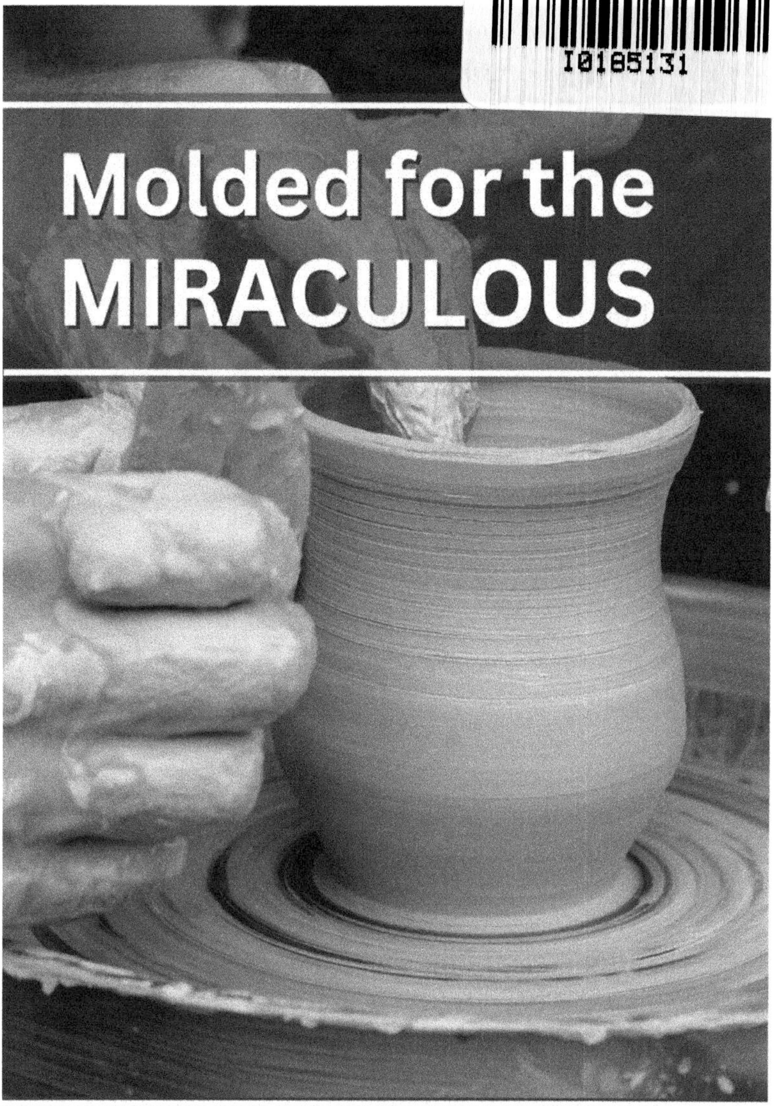

Why God Made "You"

JEANNE METCALF

1st Edition 2014
2nd Edition 2015
3rd Edition 2023

Revised 2024
Cegullah Publishing & Apologetics Academy
(CP & AA)
International Copyright © 2024
www.cegullahpublishing.ca
All rights reserved.

ISBN # Textbook: 978-1-926489-89-6
ISBN # Workbook: 978-1-926489-90-2

Cover photo © iStock # 1349271881 (2023)
Cover design by Jeanne Metcalf.

COPYRIGHT MATTERS

This book is an original manuscript by the author, protected by international copyright laws of Canada. Therefore, none of this author's work may be reproduced, in part or in whole, or stored in a retrieval system, or transmitted in any form or by any means, electronic, mechanical, photocopied, recorded or otherwise for commercial use without the *prior written* permission of the author. However, it is possible to receive permission to use short quotations for personal use, or use in a group study, or for permission to copy certain passages, or to make portions of the writings available for overhead viewing. Simply, contact the author[1] to request it.

SCRIPTURE MATTERS

All scripture quotes originate from KJV[2], public domain.
However, the name of God appears as YeHoVaH, not LORD.
See Appendix for more information.

---

[1] To contact author, see *Contact Page in Appendix*
[2] KJV King James Version. This version, when written, referred to all humankind as "mankind". When reading this version, unless the passage itself refers to a particular person, to which the text specifically refers, apply the message to all humankind, regardless of gender.

DEDICATION

I dedicate this book, first to the Living God, Yeshua Ha' Maschiach, my Lord and Saviour and secondly, to every person who is seriously interested in understanding their purpose in life and who desire to fully live it out.

May this book and its content help you to do so!!

COURSE 203

Section 1: Molded in God's Image

CHAPTER	TITLE	PAGE
1.	Made for God	9
2.	Made to Watch, Part 1	21
3.	Made to Watch, Part 2	33
4.	Made to Rest	47
5.	Made to Believe	65
6.	Made to Align	79

COURSE 204

Section 2: Molded for God's Government

7.	Made to Live	99
8.	Made to Arise	115

Section 3: Molded for God's Glory

9.	Made for His Authority	131
10.	Made for His Dominion	145
11.	Made for His Kingdom	157
12.	Made for His Purpose	171
	Conclusion	185

APPENDIX

A Name to Honour.................................	192
About Jeanne Metcalf............................	210
About the King James Version.................	198
CP & AA...	212
Contact Information...............................	212
Hebrew Root Word Index........................	204
Other Books by Jeanne Metcalf................	208
Salvation's Message................................	199
Scripture Index.......................................	205
Sinner's Prayer and Lifetime Commitment.	202

COURSE 203

SECTION 1
MOLDED IN GOD'S IMAGE

 # Made for God

"For I know the thoughts that I think toward you, says YeHoVaH, thoughts of peace, and not of evil, to give you an expected end".

Jeremiah 29:11

In the midst of a troubled nation, Israel, when the people did not understand the turmoil in the world around them, the prophet Jeremiah exclaimed that God had good thoughts or plans towards them. He desired to give them a hope, or an expected end. In other words, God had a purpose for their lives, something to bless them.

Every life has purpose, a reason for existence. Whether it is animal life, insect life, marine life, bird life, or human life, it all exists for a purpose. Humans, God's greatest creation on earth, have the most varied and wide-ranged purpose of all God's creatures. Perhaps that is why it is so difficult for many people to discover their purpose and thus fulfill their ultimate destiny.

In looking for our purpose in life, the investigation best begins with an understanding that we are *spiritual beings, and our spiritual destiny is our primary goal,* which, once in place, directs the remainder of our lives. Our ultimate spiritual destiny is heaven, enjoying eternal life with God. At least, that is God's plan for us.

In accordance with the Christian faith, we call that plan Salvation. It comes through acknowledging that we, as individuals, sin. As such, we need a Saviour. [3] Once we receive the Saviour that God provided for us, Yeshua, His Only son, our lives change. The moment we accept and receive God's plan, we step into our spiritual destiny, a destiny with corporate and individual purpose.

Corporately, we walk hand in hand with other believers on a guided path to see the fulfillment of God's plans and purposes for the earth. This is where our individual lives fit into the overall scheme of things. It is how our lives benefit the overall Body of Messiah on the earth. However, as individuals, we have an individual road to walk within that corporate setting, and we have an individual purpose.

A specific outline of our individual purpose, God defines for us as we walk day by day with Him. He

---

[3] If you are not familiar with this plan, please see Salvation's Plan in the Appendix

gives us certain gifts, which we learn to develop; individual goals to attain which we walk out one by one; and He gives us wisdom, blessings and so much more to complete His call on our life. Yet in looking at all of these things, summarizing, if you will, the entire activities of our redeemed life, we find there is still *one underlying spiritual purpose*. This purpose, when embraced, forms a foundation on which to attain every aspect of our life, spiritual and natural, corporately, and individually.

What is that underlying purpose?
How does one obtain it?

This book answers these things. It entwines both the overall corporate and individual purpose of why God put humankind upon the earth. It then explains what tools God gave to human beings to see their purpose fulfilled, and it shows, how as an individual, you can fulfill that purpose. Thus, in knowing the fundamental, spiritual purpose for which God created you, you have a choice to move towards that purpose, accept it, and live your life from that time on, with that purpose in mind.

So, let us dig into the scriptures together, and look at why God made humankind and specifically:

Why God made you!

Normally, we dig into the scriptures in the first chapter, however, here we are going to look at some important facts. [4]

    A. the original Bible transcripts
- First Testament, (Old Covenant) which we call Hebraic Scriptures because their original language was Hebrew
- New Testament, which we call Apostolic scriptures because the Apostles of Yeshua wrote them.

    B. the Ancient Hebrew Picture Language.
- Ancient Hebrew pictographs which often explain the understand original meaning of Hebrew words.

A. The Original Bible Transcripts

Since God gave the Bible to His People in a language, *other than English*, as an English-speaking person, (reader), it is important to understand that God's guarantee of Divine Inspiration applies to *the original transcripts*, not Bible translations. Ardent bible students need to realize this fact, first, and then look at the original transcripts of the Bible for clarity.

---

[4] CP & AA students. Some of this you have taken in Bible Study Basics. Use this first part, then, as a review.

However, not every Bible reader knows Hebrew, nor Greek, the languages of the Bible's ancient texts. Thus, over the years, scholars prepared materials for the average person to use as an aid to understand the meaning of the original words. Strong's Exhaustive Concordance[5] qualifies as one of those reliable sources. Its author identified all the root words of the Hebraic and Apostolic Scriptures, assigned a number to each word, and then gave a broad explanation of that word in English to help students to hopefully grasp the original message the word conveyed.

One further aid to understanding the original transcripts, more of a modern help from 21st century scholars, comes a recent discovery by scholars. These researchers of ancient historical languages uncovered an original pictograph language, which they believed was used in ancient times. This discovery further expanded upon the original concept of Hebrew Words.

While the basic meaning of many of those Hebrew words are not identical to modern Hebrew, to study these helps one to grasp some concepts of ancient meanings and thus, it gives a broader view of the deeper things deposited in the Word of God for believers.

---

[5] Strong's Concordance was first published in 1890 and is available for purchase at most Christian bookstores. It is also available for use in computer format.

Since "Molded for the Miraculous" often refers to the Ancient Pictograph Language, we included a *short explanation* on that language for the reader to review. It is only a quick overview intended to aid the student of the Word to better grasp the concept of the ancient picture language.

The Ancient Hebrew Picture Language

Whenever translating from one language to another, there is always a risk of compromising the depth of the original language, especially if that language is not as expressive as the original, and does not hold words, which precisely articulate the meaning. Such is the case when translating from Hebrew to English. For example, to translate a Hebrew 'tallit', which is an important part of the traditional Jewish garment, worn by men, we have no such English word to express it. The word 'tallit' means little tent, but the translators simply interpreted it, as 'tent'.

In our language, however, when we think of a tent, we know there are large tents and pup tents. However, 'tallit', if properly interpreted correctly refers to a large, woven shawl. Traditionally, the Hebrew people made it on a loom, using a warp and weave of white fiber. Then, when in communication with God, they wrapped this woven garment around their shoulders. Today we call that garment a prayer shawl.

Chapter 1

Can you see how translating the word, 'tallit' as 'tent', did not convey the proper meaning?

This is but one instance where early interpretations of scripture erred. Due to that one little mistake, many believers think that Acts 18:3, which described the Apostle Paul's occupation, called him a 'tentmaker". However, Paul, a Pharisee, made tallits or religious prayer shawls. This one erroneous translation teaches us not to overlook cultural expressions of the people, as well as the times and seasons when authors, inspired by God, penned the scriptures.

We must always ensure, when looking at Hebrew words with our English mind, that we consider cultural expressions as well as the times and seasons. Also, regarding the Hebrew language, we need to remember that ***Hebraic thinking differs greatly from our Western world.*** Differences in thinking, between Hebraic and Western thought, takes a lot of time to explain, so for now, keep in mind, the Hebrew language is relationally based, while most other languages are abstract. Additionally, Hebrew, like many other languages, began as an ***agriculturally based language,*** explaining ideas of their civilization with 'pictures' relative to their environment.

In this early stage of language writing skills, alphabet characters comprised of pictures with simple strokes.

Some letters indicated certain parts of the body, while others used well known animals such as the ox. These pictographs described common things during their civilization's existence.

Dr. Frank Seekins, in his book, Hebrew Word Pictures, clearly explains this aspect of early Hebrew writing. He explains, that in Hebrew pictograph language, the first letter of the alphabet, "aleph", pictured an ox's head, and the second letter "bet" represented a tent where the family lived[6]. To explain this in further detail, we will look at the word, "father", which uses both the "aleph" and the "bet".

The Hebrew Word for Father
Hebrew words usually have a base of three characters. The first two characters are known as Parent Root, the characters following are known as the Child Root. [7]

The word for father, pronounced Ab, has two major letters to make up the word. In English, we use our letters A and B. In the Hebrew they are ALEPH and BET.

---

[6] Dr. Frank Seekins in his book, "Hebrew Word Pictures" presents this agriculturally based language, clearly. ISBN 13: 978-0-967972-61-9.
[7] When understanding "Parent and Child Root" it is only in the most simplistic format that it is easy to interpret. Past four or five characters, it is more difficult to grasp.

Chapter 1   Made for God

To read those letters in English we read this way: from Left ⟶

to Right.

In Hebrew, we read this way:

⟵ from Right to Left.

For most, this seems awkward, but nevertheless keep that in mind as you read the letters on the following page:

Read from right to left

BET   ALEPH

In this picture language, the aleph once looked like an Ox's head, the bet, a simple tent, or dwelling place. The **ox** is a strong animal used to pull carts and carry heavy burdens and the like, while a tent is a base where the family lived. To read this picture, we see a strong person capable of carrying burdens, who cares for, watches over or leads the family. Hence, the Hebrew picture language describes the father as: *The strong person over the family, or to put it another way, a father is the strong one in the house.*[8]

---

[8] Dr. Seekins explains this slightly differently, however the principle of interpretation is the same.

Since the Hebrew language is relational while the English language is mostly abstract, we must learn to think differently, outside the box of the normal English mindset. When that happens, a study of Hebrew produces amazing thoughts from which we can learn much.

Proper Use of The Hebraic Picture Language
Throughout "Molded for the Miraculous", we will look at some Hebrew words where we use the agriculturally based languages as a base to obtain a deeper meaning of that Word. As you learn some of those deeper meanings, please realize that *you cannot automatically substitute that broader meaning* of that word whenever you come across the same English word in the version of scripture that you read.

When translating the Bible, scholars often used the same **English word** for **two or three different Hebrew words.** For example, in the Hebrew Scriptures, we find two major words that mean peace. One word is שלוֹם, pronounced Shalom. This word is familiar to many of us. Expanding it to the ancient picture language, it means "to break every authority causing chaos". With the absence of chaos, the result is peace. The other Hebrew word is חרשׁ, pronounced khaw-rash. This word, many do not know. Its picture in the ancient pictograph language suggests blocking words that come from the head, or in other words, it means speechless, to remain silent.

Here again is a picture of peace, but not the same in context as the first word in Hebrew, nor of our idea of peace in English. When looking at Hebrew words from the ancient, pictograph language, ensure that you observe some basic rules. Unless you are a Hebrew scholar, with a good understanding of sentence structure, only use the expanded meaning to apply to the immediate subject at hand.

Also, ensure its meaning fits well within the context of other scriptures giving reference to the same topic.

If you follow these simple rules, you should do fine!

Before closing this introduction and continuing our short discussion of the Hebrew Pictograph language, please know that the meanings of words derived from that pictograph language appear in various chapters of the book. Some Hebrew words show how their meanings were derived; however, many are left for you to explore on your own. To discover these, consider obtaining the workbook for Molded for the Miraculous. In the back of the book, in the Index, the meanings of many of these words are described in detail. The workbook is also a great way for you to use this book, and its workbook, as a Bible Study.

In closing, as we explore the scriptures together, may you, dear reader, recognize your importance to God and grasp the reason why God made you. May you see your part in the plan of things, as well as your individual destiny. May you see yourself, within the beautiful clay pot that God made you, as God see sees you, for you, truly, are:

"Molded for the Miraculous!

Made to Watch
Part 1

"My soul [waits] for the Lord more than they that watch for the morning: [I say, more than] they that watch for the morning".

Psalm 130:6

This book begins a journey in which, you dear reader, voluntarily come along. Together, we explore God's purpose for creating human beings, as well as His plans to see that purpose fulfilled. As in all journeys, we begin at the beginning, in Genesis, the bible's book of beginnings.

Genesis 1:1
1 In the beginning, God created the heaven and the earth"

Based upon the premise that God made all things, and the bible accurately records His Words, we take the first step in our journey together. If you can believe this opening verse in the bible, then dear reader, we commence our journey on this subject on common ground. However, if you cannot agree with the first words recorded for humankind, in God's love letters to His unique creation called humankind, then you may find this book too unbelievable to understand, yet alone decide to live within its principles.

Nevertheless, as we continue this journey through the pages of this book, the pavement on which we travel is the fact that from Genesis through to Revelation, the divinely inspiring writings of God to all humankind are truth, and not fiction.

With that first step settled, let us take the next step, moving forward into the book of Genesis, stopping near the end of Chapter One.

Genesis 1:27
27 So God created man in his own image, in the image of God created he him; male and female created he them.

The message here is crystal clear: *God fashioned all humanity, (including "you") in His image. Therefore, the pattern for all human interaction with God and fellow humans, God designed after His behaviour. In other words,* in all mankind's words, deeds, circumstances and situations upon the earth with Himself or others, no matter what they encountered, God designed humankind to think like and respond like Him. To see humankind interacting with God or fellow humankind then, was to see a reflection of God Himself.

Acknowledging that God designed humankind as the mirror image of Himself, let us see God's original purpose for humanity upon the earth.

Man's Purpose Before the Fall

> Genesis 2:4-8
> 4 These are the generations of the heavens and of the earth when they were created, in the day that YeHoVaH God made the earth and the heavens, 5 And every plant of the field before it was in the earth, and every herb of the field before it grew: for YeHoVaH God had not caused it to rain upon the earth, ***and there was not a man to till the ground.***[9] 6 But there went up a mist from the earth, and watered the whole face of the ground. 7 And YeHoVaH God formed man of the dust of the ground and breathed into his nostrils the breath of life; and man became a living soul. 8 And YeHoVaH God planted a garden eastward in Eden; and there he put the man whom he had formed.

A superficial read of Genesis 2:4-8 clearly denotes humanity's purpose upon the earth was "to till the

---
[9] Bold & Italics print added by the author

ground". This word "till" may describe man's care of the ground, however, it misses a deeper meaning. Taking this English interpretation as the King James Version of scripture states, we might think our purpose on the earth is always to farm, cultivate or work the land. While this denotes part of our existence on the earth, if we go to the original Hebrew text, we find there a deeper meaning, which gives a greater understanding to the subject of humankind's purpose upon the earth.

To understand the deeper meaning of the phrase, "to till the ground", let us look at two major Hebrew Words: *till* and *ground*.[10]

Hebrew Word	עבד	KJV English Word	Till
	"aw-bad"		

The pictograph language, which is the earliest form of Hebraic writings, shows something rather unique about this word. Reading from *right to left*, the first letter in this word "ע" (ayin) illustrates an eye that sees or watches. The second letter is "ב" (bet), which shows a place of residence, a home, a house, a family, or can

---

[10] Since we will look at many Hebrew words throughout this book, each Hebrew root word is presented in chart format. This makes the word under consideration easier and gives a ready reference for later.

represent the earth. These two letters make up what is called, in all Hebrew words, the parent root. This parent root informs us that the primary meaning of this word is to watch *on behalf of*[11] the place of residence, the home, the house, the family, or the earth.

The third letter, the child root, is the letter "ד" (dalet), which speaks of a doorway, entrance way or gate. Putting it all together, the expanded meaning of this word, "עבד" (aw-bad), interpreted by KJV as *"till"*, *means to watch over the earth, as a point of service, to watch on behalf of, or to keep surveillance over all doorways or points of entrance, looking for what comes forth from it.*

This fits well with the many ways which Strong's Exhaustive concordance has translate the Hebrew word, interpreting the word as to serve, 227 times, as servant 5 times, service 4 times and even giving it a spiritual connection interpreting the word as worshippers 5 times.

Keeping that thought in mind, read about the word interpreted as "ground".

Hebrew Word	אדמה	KJV English Word	Ground
	"ad-aw-mah"		

---

[11] This Hebrew word carries the idea of service and is interpreted as such in other scripture passages throughout the Word.

Before exploring this word deeper, we first note that this word contains the name by which God called the first human, "Adam". The Hebrew letters for Adam are אדם, (aleph, dalet, mem[12]). These are the same three letters in the word interpreted as "ground", אדמה (aleph, dalet, mem, heh).

That leaves only one letter difference between the word Adam and the word interpreted as ground. Therefore, as we look at the word interpreted as "ground", and the word "Adam" (which is the English pronunciation of the Hebrew word אדם), we will note similarities in their meaning.

In the ancient picture language, the letter "א" (aleph) denotes strength; the letter "ד", (dalet) [as in the word "till"], denotes a doorway; and the letter "ם", (mem) denotes "waters of life". In reference to Adam, all humankind received its life from Adam's seed, or to put it pictorially, Adam *means the strong one, the door, from whom, came the waters of life.*

The word interpreted, "ground", has one additional letter in Hebrew, the letter ה "heh". This denotes something awesome, or something victorious, and at times, can strongly suggest the breath of God present. "

---

[12] ם and מ are the same Hebrew letter known as "mem", however in Hebrew, when the letter "mem" appears at the end of the word, it changes from מ to ם.

"אדמה", interpreted *"ground"* by KJV, holds a picture *of the strong one, the door, from which comes life, and it is an awesome thing*[13]. This makes great sense, as from the "ground" comes life. Humanity indeed sustains its physical life from the ground in the food we eat, and of course the animal life that the ground also sustains.

Recapping The Meaning Of "Till the Ground"

In a practical sense, to "till the ground", within its Hebrew pictograph language, brings a picture of someone, on behalf of another, watching over the earth, looking at its doorways, in the places wherever life springs forth. This seems like a reasonable assignment, for humankind does look to the ground, planting and watching to see what comes forth. Just ask any farmer after he planted his crop. He tends to it, tenderly watches over it and cares for it to produce its good things. As a result, the farmer expects his work of service to be rewarded with an excellent harvest.

Considering, however, that humankind is a spiritual being, it makes sense too, that there follows the same idea as in the natural. So, is there a possible spiritual assignment where a person watches over the earth, looking at its doorways, looking for places where life springs forth?

---

[13] To take this one step further, God's breath present is another reference to God as the Creator of the heavens and the earth.

In spiritual terms, that is the assignment of the watchman, or intercessor. Such a person watches, first, on behalf of the One, Who appointed them in service to Him, and then on behalf of themselves and others. Now, does this purpose fit well within the context of the bible's description of a watchman or intercessor?

Let us look at the word "intercessor". In Hebrew, the word for intercessor appears in the scriptures in Isaiah 59:16[14]

Hebrew Word	פגע "paw-gah"	KJV English Word	Intercessor

Reading from *right to left*, the first letter is "פ" (pey) which carries the picture of a mouth. "ג" (gimmel), the second letter, shows a picture of a foot. These two letters forming the parent root suggests conversation, walking towards another. The child root is "ע" (ayin), the symbol of which is an eye.

Symbols, within the picture language of this word, use three parts of the body: the mouth, the foot, and the eye. Putting it all together "פגע", (paw-gah), the word KJV interprets *"intercessor"*, *pictures a "watchman"*!

---

[14] Isaiah 59:16 And he saw that there was no man, and wondered that there was no intercessor: therefore, his arm brought salvation unto him; and his righteousness, it sustained him.

today, we often use these terms synonymously. In addition, it is well worth noting that within the picture language of the word, one can see the activities of a watchman. A watchman uses the eye to see, the foot to walk about and the mouth to proclaim. These are the basic duties of a watchman.

In summary, human beings, who are God's unique and blessed creation, are thus, by God's design, "Watchmen" of the earth, both naturally and spiritually. This is a part of our service to God, and a spiritual part of our function upon the earth.

<u>Tools To Complete the Job</u>
Since God gave us a spiritual assignment to *"watch over the earth"*, then somewhere within the Word of God, it must also show us what tools He expects us to utilize to complete the task. To those ends, then, let us continue our journey through the Word of God, this time looking back at Genesis One to see any clues given at the time of creation.

In Genesis 1 we read:

> Genesis 1:26-28
> 26 And God said, Let us make man in our image, after our likeness: and let them have ***dominion***[15] over the fish of the sea, and over the fowl of the air,

---
[15] Italics and bold lettering by author.

and over the cattle, and over all the earth, and over every creeping thing that creepeth upon the earth. 27 So God created man in his own image, in the image of God created he him; male and female created he them. 28 And God blessed them, and God said unto them, **Be fruitful, and multiply**, and ***replenish*** the earth, and ***subdue it***: and have dominion over the fish of the sea, and over the fowl of the air, and over every living thing that moveth upon the earth.

First, notice that God gave humankind *"dominion"* over the fish of the sea, the fowl of the air, the cattle, over every creeping thing, and over all the earth. This is one tool given to humankind. While the Bible calls it dominion, believers mistakenly call it "authority". Yet dominion, when properly understood, wields authority.

To grasp the total concept and therefore, understand exactly what God means, let us see the Hebrew word in its primary picture language. This helps to explain the depth of the word, KJV interpreted, "dominion".

Hebrew Word	רדה "raw-daw"	KJV English Word	dominion

Reading from right to left, the letters are "ר" (resh), "ד" (dalet), and "ה" (heh). The first letter indicates the supreme position as "head", and the second letter "ד"

(dalet), indicates a doorway, entrance way or gate. Without even going into the child root, we see that the parent root shows, that to have dominion, a Leader rules (or has authority) over the doorways, or entrance points to admit or refuse entrance by others. The child root, "הֿ"(heh), indicates victory.

Here we have it: a marvellous picture of *"dominion" depicting the authoritative tool of rulership or headship, over all doorways, which establishes a person as victorious.* Here we see not only the authoritative tool, but also, God's intentions that humankind stand victorious in his task of *"watching over the doorways of the earth"*, all of which is done in service to the living God fulfilling His command.

This scripture in Genesis gives us an important factor that we cannot overlook. God intended humankind to walk *in great authority* on the earth and *to rule* the earth. God created humanity for victory while upon the earth. He never created us for defeat. We see that same thinking also, in the very name God gave to His first human created, namely Adam.

Hebrew Word	אדם "aw-dawm"	KJV English Word	Adam

Earlier, you saw that this word "אדם" (Adam) and "", אדמה (pronounced "ad-aw-mah") which KJV interpreted ground, have similar letters. When we examined the word for ground, we expounded on the name Adam, and we said that Ada*m means the strong one, the door from whom, come the waters of life.* While Adam is, without doubt, the first human being, the word itself also indicates strength *and continuation of existence.* God intended man as victorious over all things, including death.

In the commission to Adam, in the word "dominion", strong evidence exists to show that God gave Adam *continued headship, or dominion, over all things in the earth* including animal life within the sea and flying above in the heavens. God endowed Adam *and his wife,* who came from him, with *dominion.* Had this couple remained in the state of innocence as before their fall, that dominion would then pass on or continue to be upon all their offspring.

This theme, we will pick up in the next chapter, Made to Watch, Part 2, and will recap both chapters at the chapter end.

Made to Watch
Part 2

"Therefore YeHoVaH God sent him (Adam) forth from the garden of Eden, to till the ground from whence he was taken."

Genesis 3:23

Further Evidence of Authority To Rule

Prior to the record of the fall, God makes it clear that He fashioned human beings in His Image, and then Genesis 1: 28[16] further declared, **"Be fruitful, and multiply**, and **replenish** the earth, and **subdue it"**.

Obviously, from these words, God shows us that He desired this first couple to *increase their own kind*, and in that increase, they *"replenish the earth"*. However, the word "replenish', in English does not do justice to the Hebrew root word.

---

[16] Genesis 1:28 And God blessed them, and God said unto them, **Be fruitful, and multiply**, and **replenish** the earth, and **subdue it**: and have dominion over the fish of the sea, and over the fowl of the air, and over every living thing that moveth upon the earth.

Hebrew Word	מָלֵא "maw-lay"	KJV English Word	replenish

Using the picture language, we see a much deeper meaning.

"מ" (mem), indicates the waters of life, humankind and the like. "ל" (lamed) shows a strength to pull into order, and the last letter, the child root, "א" (aleph), means a powerful, pulling force, which can be supreme.

The overall picture shows that the word KJV interpreted "replenish", indicates the waters of life continuing, the eminent victory of existence of humankind. While *replenish* seems to be a good word indicating an increase of humanity, it somehow misses the concept of the continuation of life, which God intended to *conquer all that rises up against it.*

That Hebrew root word, in its original picture language, shows that continuation of life and, once again, strengthens the concept of "dominion". That same concept follows through with the next word in verse 28, "כבש" interpreted as "subdue".

Hebrew Word	כבש "kaw-bash"	KJV English Word	subdue

This word KJV translated *"subdue"* presents a picture of *a hand* coming towards a person, home, or nation *with an ability to devour it, or at the very least, bring it into bondage.*

From these few scriptures and words just expanded upon, it shows that God fully intended humankind to rule, or walk in complete dominion, upon the earth. We can also perceive a permanence or eternal factor here. God made humankind to continue, both in fellowship with Him, and each other, as well as a continuation to enjoy life upon the earth.

Death, from eternity past to eternity future, *does not originate from God's kingdom,* nor was it part of God's design for humankind to experience.

God's intentions for the first Adam and his wife show up in their assignment as "watchman" over the earth's doorways, with the authority of the dominion whereby He commissioned them. As natural watchmen, before the fall, humankind's[17] purpose, as designed by God, was to implement their authority and subdue any actions upon the earth which acted contrary to *bringing forth life.*

---

[17] Whenever you see this term "man", please remember it refers to all humankind.

In other words, God appointed Adam and his wife as Watchmen, to keep God's order in the earth, to ensure God's kingdom reigned upon the earth, including His will for Life to continue upon the earth. Since the first couple created by God were also a spiritual entity, their commission, and its inherent authority, covered all needed activities in a spiritual world as well.

The Fall

Behind this scene of the fall, the bible describes a "spiritual enemy or adversary" that despised their position, power, authority, and dominion upon the earth. After their spiritual adversary surfaced, convinced the woman to eat the fruit and the woman invited Adam to follow suit, Adam then disobeyed God and ate the forbidden fruit. Paul describes the aspects of the fall in this manner:

1 Timothy 2:14
14 and Adam was not deceived, but the woman being deceived was in the transgression.

Adam, unlike his wife who was deceived, disobeyed God. He clearly understood right from wrong in that situation, yet he refused to comply with God's command. His disobedience opened a door affecting all that lived upon the earth. From that point onward, the earth and its diverse inhabitants became subject to death, when earlier, before Adam's disobedience, the earth, and all living upon it, knew only life. The book of Romans puts it this way:

> Romans 5:12
> 12 Wherefore, as by one man sin entered into the world, and death by sin; and so death passed upon all men, for that all have sinned:

Adam did not comply with the will of God but rather, made a choice independent of God's desire for humankind.

Life in the Garden, prior to the fall, operated as an environment patterned after God's kingdom. When Adam sinned, he opened the door to the entrance of death, and thus, a conflict arose with God's original design. Adam, God's creation, designed to rule over the earth and all life from it, then became subject to live in a lesser state than that which God created. This *fallen state* created through sin, received a death's blow and thus, from Adam onward, every human being inherited "death". Unfortunately, not only all human life knew death, but the animals on the earth became subject to death, too.

Keep in mind that, while "death" invaded humankind's spiritual and physical well being, and through Adam's disobedience, all humankind lost the authority, power and ability to walk in dominion over the earth, **death did not destroy** *God's ultimate plans!* God desires all humankind to live with Him eternally. As tragic and as horrible as the situation appeared, God planned restoration, *but on His terms!*

After The Fall

God sent the first couple out of the garden of Eden.[18] In doing so, He reinforced the original purpose given:

> Genesis 3:23
> 23 Therefore YeHoVaH God sent him (Adam) forth from the garden of Eden, to till the ground from whence he was taken.

Once again, that word "עבד" ("aw-bad"), interpreted as "till", clearly designated that this couple shall watch over the earth for what it produces, including the watch over the earth, keeping surveillance over its doorways or points of entrance.

While the purpose here still focuses on the "watching", the authority, which God gave them, was missing.

> That authority's absence did not change their original purpose; however, it affected how that purpose would find its fulfillment.

---

[18] The Hebrew Pictograph for Eden shows Ayin, an eye, Dalet, a door, and Noon, a seed. Together it presents a picture of watching over the doorway, to receive an inheritance.

This absence posed a large problem. If they could not successfully watch over the earth before the fall, how could they complete the task after the fall, when death ruled? The answer is simple. They simply could not.

If the decision to *disobey God* came by an *independent* choice, it follows then that *obeying God* comes by a **continued decision** to *depend upon God* to help in keeping His will.

Watching over the earth, in the best possible way, could only happen with God's help.

That help came when this first couple humbled themselves before God, accepted His Ways, believing and receiving His Way of Salvation, and then, by God's strength, complete their assignments on earth as they lived out the length of their days.

Knowing this, how did their children fair?

God And Cain
Genesis speaks of a day when Cain and Abel, the first male offspring of Adam and Eve, brought an offering to the Lord.

Genesis 4:5-7
5 But unto Cain and to his offering he had not respect. And Cain was very wroth, and his countenance fell. 6 And YeHoVaH said unto Cain,

Why art thou wroth? and why is thy countenance fallen? 7 If thou doest well, shalt thou not be accepted? and if thou doest not well, **sin lieth at the door**. And unto thee shall be his desire, and thou shalt rule over him.

The bottom line to these two offerings lies in this fact: *we know from the type of offering, spoken of throughout scripture, that Abel brought a "sin-offering". With that offering, he pleased God.*

Without going into too much detail, biblical commentators believe that when God killed an animal to make clothes for Adam and Eve, He showed them salvation's plan through the slain animal, a lamb. From that lamb, God made them clothes.

Genesis 3:20-23

20 And Adam called his wife's name Eve, because she was the mother of all living. 21 Unto Adam also and to his wife did YeHoVaH God make coats of skins and clothed them. 22 And YeHoVaH God said, Behold, the man is become as one of us, to know good and evil: and now, lest he put forth his hand, and take also of the tree of life, and eat, and live for ever: 23 Therefore YeHoVaH God sent him forth from the garden of Eden, to till the ground from whence he was taken.

Knowing then, that Adam knew the required "sin-offering", it follows that he taught their two sons. Thus, we have the two sons bringing their offering before YeHoVaH. Cain, however, did not present a sin offering, but a grain offering from the ground which Cain grew his crops. In Genesis 4:7, God speaks to Cain about this offering, which he brought:

Genesis 4:7-8
    7 If thou doest well, shalt thou not be accepted? and if thou doest not well, sin lieth at the door. And unto thee shall be his desire, and thou shalt rule over him. 8 And Cain talked with Abel his brother: and it came to pass, when they were in the field, that Cain rose up against Abel his brother, and slew him.

Cain was in trouble. Sin lay at the door.

In the Hebrew, **there is a picture of a crouching animal, in an attack position, ready to spring through the door.** Cain, for his own sake, needed to bring a sin offering. If he had done so, he, by his very actions, would acknowledge that he was in trouble regarding his attitude towards his brother, Abel, and in need of God's help.

Since Abel kept the flock of animals, from which Cain must find his lamb for a sin offering, Cain must first mend the rift between his brother and himself.

Unfortunately, Cain did not do that, but when he brought a grain offering, which he produced with his own hands, he bypassed any relationship mending with his brother, Abel. Understanding Cain's heart in this matter, the Lord warns Cain "sin lies at the door". If Cain had watched the door, as God advised, then Cain would avert sin's desire to rule him and, by dealing with the sin, leaning on God for help, he would assert his rulership over sin. Obviously, Cain did not watch this door, nor reach out to God for help, but rather ignored God's warning and shortly thereafter, killed his brother, Abel.

Watching And Sin
This theme of "watching over the doorways", enlarges a bit in the example of Cain, where it brings the "watching" close to home in that each person must carefully watch over their own life, to ensure the desires of sin not have dominion over them. If they find sin the victor, God has provided a remedy, which humankind is free to accept or reject.

That remedy, of course, is to take the path, which leads to an open door to "salvation, which humankind has known since Adam sinned[19]. Moving further past

---

[19] Under the First Covenant, they knew Salvation's plan, by repentance and obedience to bring a sin offering. In the New Covenant, we know the sin-offering foreshadowed Yeshua on the cross

Genesis, we see this watching theme again, but this time it comes as a warning from Yeshua, as He spoke to His disciples.

Matthew 26:40-41
> 40 And he[20] came unto the disciples, and found them asleep, and said unto Peter, What, could you not watch with me one hour? 41 **Watch and pray, that you enter not into temptation:** the spirit indeed [is] willing, but the flesh [is] weak".

Yeshua admonishes His disciples that watching and praying brings an alertness, to monitor the desires of the flesh, for these can present problems, if not ruled by the Spirit. God expects mankind to live a life pleasing to Him, in which we focus, not on sin and satisfying our fleshing desires, but on what pleases God. Remember, God made us in His Image and our thoughts, words and deeds are to reflect His!

There is one last "watch", which refers to a reproving and it comes in the book of Habakkuk.

Habakkuk 2:1
> 1 I will stand upon my watch, and set me upon the tower, and will watch to see what he will say unto me, and what I shall answer when I am reproved.

---

[20] Yeshua

Here, the prophet stands upon the place of his watch and states his awareness that "reproving" or "correction" comes from God, and so, he will watch for it. Then, once received, Habakkuk will respond. The theme of "watching" over the "doors" for sin's entrance continues from Genesis onward, into the New Testament. It is an important aspect of our human existence.

In Summary
Summarizing the first purpose of humankind as outlined in Genesis, then, *before and after the fall*, we see that God made man *to watch*. To do that task, prior to the fallen, God gave the first man, Adam, and his wife, Eve, authority in which to rule with dominion, commissioning them to subdue or bring into bondage, whatsoever threatened to act contrary to God's will.

Adam failed in this task, even though fully equipped to stand against the wiles of "ha satan",[21] he disobeyed and opened the door to sin and death. That choice led to a loss of total authority over all the earth and brought about an expulsion from the garden. At which time God reinforced, rather than changed their purpose on the earth: *to watch over the doorways of the earth*. That doorway pictures or represents the many events and

---

[21] The adversary

encounters humankind experiences daily and indicates their needed response.

Human beings, therefore, God created as watchers over the earth, over their own lives and those of others, as well as the events which transpire upon the earth. God calls humankind to remain awake, alert, and ready to respond to whatever threats arise to make life here like the power of Darkness and unlike the "Kingdom of God".

Our task, *when fulfilled responsibly*, takes the necessary measures to bring the Kingdom of God into our own life and, at the same time, gives opportunity to learn how *to overrule the power of Darkness*. While humankind lost their dominion, God planned for its restoration and in the meantime, God provided victory for His creation through His mercy and grace.

As humankind watches[22] over these doorways before us, we observe, consider and act in response to whatever these things try to bring into our life. God desires, when we respond to situations that we encounter on this earth, that we align with His Will,

---

[22] Watching. Waiting. Warning, brings explains the principle of watching, in greater depth. ISBN# Textbook: 978-1-926489-80-3; Prayerbook: 978-1-926489-81-0; Workbook: 978-1-926489-82-7

thus ***not answering*** *temptation's call,* but rather *His call* to live righteously before His Face.

By this activity of watching, humankind lives in a capacity greater than a simply a caretaker of the earth. Clearly, God made humankind a "watcher". Each "watcher", while operating within a biblical format, keeps their own uniqueness and importance as an individual. On that note, please remember, that God never loses sight of our individuality! Beloved do not lose sight of your individuality or uniqueness, either!

 **Made to Rest**

"And he said, My presence shall go with thee, and I will give thee rest".

Exodus 33:14

Now that you know that God designed every human being to first "watch" over their life, and then "watch" over the happenings on the earth, you may ask, "how does one goes about watching?" "Molded for the Miraculous", presents principles on how to watch to help the reader understand a needed foundation for watching, and thus to fulfil their purpose of watching. The final Chapter, then, returns to the theme of watching.

So, in this chapter, we will look at watching from the perspective of resting in God. Before going in that direction, however, we will look at the time immediately after the fall to outline some of the challenges the fall brought to humankind.

After the fall in the Garden of Eden, to ensure that things on the earth happened God's way, it became more difficult than ever, to fulfill the command to watch, because the earth suffered a change.

> Genesis 3:17-20
> 17 And unto Adam he said, Because thou hast hearkened unto the voice of thy wife, and hast eaten of the tree, of which I commanded thee, saying, Thou shalt not eat of it: cursed is the ground for thy sake; in sorrow shalt thou eat of it all the days of thy life; 18 Thorns also and thistles shall it bring forth to thee; and thou shalt eat the herb of the field; 19 In the sweat of thy face shalt thou eat bread, till thou return unto the ground; for out of it wast thou taken: for dust thou art, and unto dust shalt thou return. 20 and Adam called his wife's name Eve; because she was the mother of all living.

God "cursed" the ground[23] and now thorns and thistles sprang from it. The English word KJV interpreted "curse" however, misses something that the Hebrew word reveals. "ארר" ("aw-rar"), interpreted by KJV as curse, in the ancient picture language, shows something dominant, a pulling force, which becomes supreme, and then rules. The ground, from the words God spoke to it, transformed to a state where it now freely, without effort, produced thorns and thistles, however, its production of food to support human life

---
[23] Please note: God did not curse humankind!

humankind would no longer come forth on its own. Humankind must now labour for it.

To look at the ground and growing things, we know it does not come from the ground on its own today, *except for weeds*. Looking in places where humankind does not inhabit the land and care for it, wild conditions exist. Unless attended, lands become wild or unkept. Cultivating takes effort, especially to rid areas of weeds.

Our forests, also become overgrown with wild vines, wild plants, etc. This overgrowth comes as a direct result of the fall, but rarely do we think of it in that way. We should remember that the ground, as it produces thorns, thistles, and countless challenges to humankind, were never part of God's original design for it or for humankind. These were simply not part of His perfect will for the earth. It came because of sin.

Additional Problems to Consider

Now that humankind lived in a sinful state, in a changed world, the task of "watching over the doorways of the earth", meant greater difficulty than before, not just physically, but also spiritually. After Adam disobeyed and thus, opened the door to sin and death, to see God's will and kingdom come into every situation, he, his wife and sons battled the effects of sin and death.

Unfortunately, just as it was easier for the earth to produce thorns and thistles than crops, it was easier for humankind *to bend towards sin*, than follow the ways of God.

The more humankind bent towards sin, the more the image of God in humankind disappeared too.

In the early beginnings after the fall, we saw that Cain hated his brother Abel and refused God's counsel to deal with that hatred. Instead, he allowed sin to rule him, and then, with sin leading him, Cain killed his brother, Abel. That action violated humankind's original purpose set in place by God on the earth, and at the same time, marred the image of God in Cain's life. Cain, instead, expressed the image of sin, powered by Darkness[24].

Nevertheless, God did not change the assigned task to "watch" over the earth and in doing so, express His Nature and character upon the earth. Yet, as we read from Genesis onward, we cannot find one person who did that task with a success rate of 100%. We have

---

[24] After Cain killed Abel, YeHoVaH said unto Cain, "Where is Abel thy brother? And he said I know not: Am I my brother's keeper?" (Genesis 4:9) Considering that humankind's God-ordained purpose includes to "watch" over the lives of others (especially their family), as well as their own, in order to ensure God's kingdom comes and His will is done, God does indeed see us as our brother's keeper.

various degrees of that success, but only one person ever completed that task to perfection. That person, of course, was Yeshua.

All saints, who lived prior to Yeshua, acknowledged their need for God to help them, and by their walk with God, they accomplished their God-assigned task of "watching" to whatever degree they found it possible, utilizing God's help of course. Those who pleased God were those who, by faith, walked with God. Saints, since Yeshua, followed the same protocol as those prior to the cross, and with the help God, also live their lives by faith, and by that, complete their assigned task of "watching", to the best of their ability.

New Covenant saints, however, have an easier task than did saints before the cross. Being born again[25] aligns a believer for an implant of God's Spirit within them, and thus, once deposited, the Holy Spirit makes it possible for God's image to shine through the believer. This is in keeping with the Apostle Peter's statement when he referred to believers as partakers of God's Divine Nature.

2 Peter 1:4
   4 Whereby are given unto us exceeding great and precious promises: that by these ye *might be*

---

[25] Some call the Salvation experience as born again, or born from above, or born of God's Spirit. Read John 3:5 to 8

partakers of the divine nature, having escaped the corruption that is in the world through lust.

For those who wish to walk with God today, we do so by entering through the door of Salvation, through Yeshua, Who is the door. As we enter, we rest in the finished works done on the cross on our behalf. From then on, this new life which begun by faith continues as we learn to live by faith, day by day.

In other words, we live a ***life of faith*** in which we continue to remain at rest[26] in the fulfilled works of the cross. From that place of resting in God, we learn to fulfill our call to "watch over the doorways of the earth" and endeavour to walk in God's kingdom and fulfill His will[27].

A Life of Faith
Regarding the life of faith, Habakkuk, the prophet spoke these words:

Habakkuk 2:4
> 4 Behold, his soul [which] is lifted up is not upright in him: but the just shall live by his faith.

---

[26] Hebrews 3:11-18 speaks of entering God's rest. This principle we look at more detail later on in this chapter.

[27] John 10: 7 Then said Jesus unto them again, Verily, verily, I say unto you, I am the door of the sheep. 8 All that ever came before me are thieves and robbers: but the sheep did not hear them. 9 I am the door: by me if any man enter in, he shall be saved, and shall go in and out, and find pasture.

In this scripture in Habakkuk[28], we have two types of people: unsaved and saved. In addition, we see the major difference between these two types of people recorded. We have summarized these in chart form below.

Two Types Shown in Habakkuk 2:4	
UNSAVED	*SAVED (Redeemed)*
"Behold, his soul which is lifted up, is not upright in him",	"The just shall live by faith",
INDICATION	**INDICATION**
This part of Habakkuk 2:4 indicates someone whose **heart** is filled with pride.	This part of Habakkuk 2:4 indicates a person who God calls **"just"**, or in modern vernacular, "saved".
COMMENTS ABOUT THE UNSAVED	**COMMENTS ABOUT THE SAVED**
From that heart of pride, these people direct their lives. Such people boast, "I did it my way!" These people follow the pull of their heart.	These people trust the Lord and live by the principles that please God. These live by faith.

---

[28] The latter part of the verse, "the just shall live by faith", writers in the New Testament, stressed its importance by recording it three times. Romans 1:17; Galatians 3:11; Hebrews 10:38

Major Difference:
The difference between the two types lies in the attitude of the heart, from which people make life decisions. • The unsaved person, whose heart is prideful, God classified as "not upright". • The saved person chooses to walk with God, doing it God's way, which is a life of "faith". Only a humble heart depends upon God.

Both types of people respond from their heart. The saved person humbles himself or herself before God, knowing their vindication with God does not happen by their own merits. On the other hand, the prideful person embraces the thought, *"I did it my way"*. Unfortunately, pride, originating in the heart, deceived that person! Regarding this subject and its rudimentary affect upon a person, the prophet Obadiah wrote:

Obadiah 1:3
> 3 "The pride of thine heart hath deceived thee, thou that dwellest in the clefts of the rock, whose habitation [is] high; that saith in his heart, Who shall bring me down to the ground?"

Obadiah spoke this word to Edom, a nation whose major cities lay deep within the mountains. Thus, they thought themselves impenetrable and boasted of their invincibility. While this scripture referred to the nation, the concept within the scripture applies to individuals, stressing the fact that "pride of heart" will deceive you.

Deception misleads, tricks, even betrays its victims. Edom, an ancient nation spoken of in the scripture above, thought no one could possibly overcome them. They thought they would remain fortified forever. For various just reasons, one of which was unrepented pride, God's judgment necessitated their conquest. After He put His plans in motion, Edom became a defeated nation, just as God predicted.

Why did their arrogant boast of invincibility fall to the ground? From where did the deception of their impenetrability, stem? According to the passage in Obadiah, which you just read, this arrogance stemmed from within their heart. Obadiah spoke about it to Edom, and other prophets like Jeremiah said it to others:

Jeremiah 17:9
9 "The heart [is] deceitful above all [things], and desperately wicked: who can know it?"

Jeremiah further elaborates on the subject, to help us understand how to avoid our heart deceiving us. That information we glean by understanding some key words in Jeremiah 17:9, namely heart, deceitful, and desperately wicked.

The Heart

Hebrew Word	לֵבָב	KJV English Word	Heart
	"lay-bawb" or "lev"		

Reading from right to left, the first letter is "ל", lamed. The early pictograph letter designates control, pulling or yoking something. It can also mean to teach in the sense of leading or correcting. The next letter "ב", bet, indicates the place of residence, such as the body, home, house, family, nation, or earth. The third letter is the letter "ב" bet, repeated. Here the picture shows that *the heart is something that leads or controls the person.* There is a strong indication that *the "heart" instructs* a person by giving out ideas and suggestions on ways to do things. This leadership pleases the desires of "self".

Hebrew Word	עָקֹב	KJV English Word	Deceitful
	"aq-ab"		

"ע" ayin, the first letter, shows eyes watching, looking ahead, experiencing something. "ק", kof, pictures a sun coming from over the horizon, symbolizing that which is beyond one's control. The final letter, "ב" bet, speaks of the place of residence, the home, the body, etc. This word, "deceitful", when recapped in its picture language, means *to see, look towards, or long for something beyond oneself, in order to experience, or know it.* What it seeks goes beyond what God designed for humankind to experience. In searching for it, it appears different in the beginning from the fruit it eventually produces.

Hebrew Word	אנש "aw-nash"	KJV English Word	Desperately wicked

"א" aleph, denotes a strength, pulling strongly, etc. "נ" noon, suggests an inheritance, such as children (mankind's inheritance), sown by the "seed of life". The "ש" shin, pictures a mighty, destructive force. In overall pictograph images, the word KJV interpreted as *"desperately wicked", indicates a strong force, depositing its seed, (its form of life), which goes on). The result of this is destruction, or ruin.*

The Heart According to The Bible

Jeremiah's words in Chapter 17: 9[29] have great depth of meaning. Summed up, this scripture tells us that the

---

[29] "The heart is deceitful above all things, and desperately wicked: who can know it?"

heart, *(which is the force that controls, pulls, or guides the person)*, longs for something beyond itself, so it can know or experience it, and as such, is a strong force producing an inheritance (or results of an action) which is destructive.

To recap these thoughts from Habakkuk, Obadiah, and Jeremiah,

The heart is a strong, controlling force within the person, well able to deceive that person as to its intentions, projecting its desires upon them as the right thing to do. The longings and desires of the heart lead, or pull, the person into areas where God's perfect will does not intend that person to go. The results of the choices made, (or the inheritance resulting from those choices) is ruin.

The book of Proverbs agrees with this conclusion.

> Proverbs 14:12
> 12 There is a way, which seems right unto a man, but the end thereof are the ways of death.

The words in Habakkuk 2:4, *""Behold, his soul which is lifted up, is not upright in him"* relate a *very* sad state of affairs. In contrast, the remaining part of the verse gives great hope for the "just". A look at that Hebrew word is enlightening.

Hebrew Word	[30] צָדִיק "tsad-deek"	KJV English Word	Just

"צָד", (tsade & dalet) form the parent root. It shows someone resting yet entering a doorway. " יק " (yod and qof), suggest work from above. *A "just person", as depicted in early picture language, is someone who, rests in works that come from above in every situation that they encounter.* This word picture of a "just" person is accurate and lines up with the message from the author of the book of Hebrews:

Hebrews 4:3
> 3 For we which have believed do enter *into rest*, as he said, As I have sworn in my wrath if they shall enter *into my rest*: **although the works were finished from the foundation of the world.**

A person who is "just", is one who believes, and then receives the works of God provided for them.

Such a person knows there is nothing they can add with their own ideas or works, they need only accept YeHoVaH's provisions, and then *"rest"* in those finished works, which God finished before the

---

[30] From this point on, we will only sum up the picture meaning.

foundation of the world. These just (saved) believers put "faith" to work on their behalf.

On this topic, the author of the book of Hebrew says:

> Hebrews 4:1-2
> 1 Let us therefore fear, lest a promise being left us of *entering into his rest*, any of you should seem to come short of it. 2 For unto us was the gospel preached, as well as unto them: but the word preached did not profit them, *not being mixed with faith in them that heard it.*

When one "rests" in the works of God, they walk *by faith*. Entering God's rest, they learn to "watch".

Just as Hebrew 4:2 states, the gospel only profits those who, when they hear it, mix it with faith. The author of Hebrews goes on to say:

> Hebrews 11:6
> 6 But without faith it is impossible to please him: for he that comes to God must believe that he is, and that he is a rewarder of them that diligently seek him.

Regarding "salvation", God did it beforehand and so today's believers receive the work of the cross, *yet* according to the book of Revelation, the work of our salvation followed a finished work of YeHoVaH:

Revelation 13:7-8
> 7 And it was given unto him to make war with the saints, and to overcome them: and power was given him over all kindreds, and tongues, and nations. 8 And all that dwell upon the earth shall worship him, whose names are not written in the book of life of ***the Lamb slain from***[31] ***the foundation of the world.***

Yeshua's work that He accomplished on the cross was finished earlier, prior to or before the foundation of the world.

As Yeshua walked the earth, He *believed His Father for the work God sent Him to do. Knowing that work His Father made possible, Yeshua rested* in *those finished works,* and thus hand in hand with the Father, produced for all humankind, the Salvation God prepared earlier before the foundation of the world.

Yes, Yeshua, the perfect Son of God, the Word of God incarnate, walked by *"faith" principles* in His life on earth, and in doing so, pleased God. He is our example too, and all those who believe in Yeshua enter their walk by faith *with Him,* accepting the work already

---

[31] "from" can also be interpreted as "before".

done for them by God on the cross, knowing that, on their own, they can neither earn righteousness, nor procure their own salvation.

After our initial day of salvation, we walk out our life resting in that which God provided for us. In other words, we *enter our rest as we live by faith*. These two aspects of our Christian walk intricately connect. Therefore, we will look more at faith in the next chapter. For now, remember that by entering God's rest, you received your salvation. After salvation, you learn to live in that rest and from that position, walk out your life[32].

In Summary
A heart filled with pride; God does not consider upright. One, who God calls "just", on the other hand, humbly accepts God's plans for their life, accepting by faith, the finished works God provided for them. Faith, then, begins a believer's walk with God, and transpires throughout every aspect of their life from salvation onward. "Resting in God's finished works" is an important concept for all believers as, by faith, they enter the Kingdom of God at Salvation, as redeemed souls.

---

[32] Remember, the just shall live by faith. Habakkuk 2:4

Faith, which partners with rest in God's finished works, becomes the pathway on which believers begin and then continue their walk with God.

Beloved, learn and enjoy that faith walk by entering your rest throughout your Christian life. This pleases God and reaps great rewards!

 **Made to Believe**

"Even as Abraham believed God, and it was accounted to him for righteousness".

Galatians 3:6

As previously discussed in the last chapter, once we believe we enter our rest. Thus, through believing, our faith opens a wide door to our relationship with God to receive salvation's benefit as well as what awaits us in our walk with God. Faith, intricately woven with rest, becomes the highway, on which we travel in our walk with God. Therefore, in this chapter, we will look at faith's perspective.

When speaking of faith, the book of Hebrew says:

Hebrews 11:1
1 Now faith is the substance of things hoped for, the evidence of things not seen.

KJV interpreted the Greek Word, υποστασις "hoop-os'-tas-is" as "substance". This word normally speaks of *"something under another thing"*, such as the foundation, which sits under a building.

Foundations are groundwork to support buildings, and the strength and durability of the building depends upon the integrity of its foundation. If resting upon a faulty foundation, a building will not last. If the foundation is strong and true, however, the building, when properly structured, stands for a long time.

In the same way, as Christian believers, our strong and true foundation of "faith" gives us a solid base upon which to live our lives. In other words, faith gives us a concrete foundation, which supports us securely through all the circumstances we encounter upon this earth.

Our decisions in life, therefore, *if based upon "faith"*, provide an excellent *foundation* for living. Since decisions, according to Hebrew thought, come from the "heart" and not the "head", **we need to understand how to help the "heart" decide to live by "faith"**. The best way to understand is to **compare the Hebrew word for "heart" to the Hebrew word for "faith"**.

The Hebrew Word: Faith
To keep the consistency of scripture, we will look at the Hebrew word for faith as found in Habakkuk 2:4, "the

just shall live by *faith"*, which scripture we looked at briefly, before.

Hebrew Word	אמונה	KJV English Word	Faith[33]
	"em-oo-naw"		

"אמ" form the parent root. Note that the ancient picture language shows the word KJV interpreted as *"faith", is a strong, drawing type of leadership, helping one to overcome life's issues, and as such it attaches itself to a person to bring all works and deeds to complete surrender to follow faith's leadership.*

> In connection to God, the leadership which faith gives, joins with the things of the Spirit of God. Faith's job, therefore, brings us into alignment with God's Will and His Kingdom. Thus, faith, when possessed by the heart, pleases God.

Couple this definition with the fact that "faith", *if given opportunity*, forms a believer's foundation. Now, we have reason to grasp the chief and most effective component in which to walk through life with God as our Lord and Saviour. Our part, as God made us to believe, means we embrace the concept of faith,

---

[33] To see the exact way this meaning was derived, please see the workbook.

welcome it, agree with it, and implement it. God's part gives birth to faith's goals, and thus, we receive them.

As the author to the Corinthians said:

> 2 Corinthians 1:20
> 20 For all the promises of God in him are yea, and in him Amen, unto the glory of God by us.

Comparison of Two Hebrew Words: Heart & Faith

Knowing then, that God designed "faith" as a powerful leader for our lives, how do we embrace and implement faith? Comparing that Hebrew word KJV interpreted faith, (אמונה "em-oo-naw") with the Hebrew word KJV interpreted as heart, broadens our understanding.

Using the explanation of the picture language for the words heart and faith, as previously related, we easily identify the leadership qualities of each of these two words, as well as the direction and focus of their leadership. The following chart puts the two words and their picture meanings, side by side.

(See the Charts on the next page)

COMPARISON OF TWO HEBREW WORDS: HEART & FAITH	
HEART	FAITH
The ancient picture language shows that *the heart is something that leads or controls the person.*	*Faith is a **strong, drawing type of leadership, helping** one to overcome life's issues, and as such, it attaches itself to a person, to bring all works and deeds to complete surrender to follow its leadership.*

DIRECTION OF LEADERSHIP	
HEART	FAITH
There is a strong indication that *the "heart" tutors* a person by giving out ideas and suggestions on ways to do things.	In connection to God, the leadership connects with things of the Spirit of God, which bring us into alignment with His Will and His Kingdom.

FOCUS	
HEART	FAITH
Leads by intentions to please self	Leads by the Holy Spirit to follow the will of God and therefore pleases God

The human heart:
- as a powerful leader, takes its owner into realms of *temporal value,* which satisfy self.

Faith:
- as a powerful leader, on the other hand, brings its owner into a relationship with God, which of course benefits the person in its promises of *eternal value.*

In other words, a person first needs to appreciate the eternal value of a relationship with God, *over the temporal value of self-satisfaction* and then, make a decision *(which originates in the heart)* to allow "faith" to lead them. The deciding factor then, to which leadership rules, is the person's choice.

Paul, in his letter to the Romans wrote:

Romans 10:8 b) - 10
8 b The word is nigh thee, even in thy mouth, and in thy heart: that is, *the word of faith,* which we preach; 9 That if thou shalt confess with thy mouth the Lord Jesus, and **shalt believe in thine heart** that God hath raised him from the dead, **thou shalt be saved.** 10 For with the **heart man believeth** unto righteousness; and with the mouth confession is made unto salvation.

Faith deposits itself within the heart when a person hears the Word of God preached. That person, then, believes in their heart what they heard to be true, (in this case from Romans 10:8, salvation procured by Yeshua, which brings righteousness), and next, they speak their choice to others.

> **When a person operates their life from a faith foundation, they exchange the leadership of their heart for the leadership of faith[34].**

Under the First Covenant, this is how it worked, and under the New Covenant, it still works the same way, *only in this covenant, believers have a greater benefit:* believers receive, at salvation, a new heart, which longs for the things of God. This, God promised to do through First Covenant prophets and fulfilled that promise under the New Covenant. Hebrews confirms this.

> Hebrews 8:8 b-10
> 8 b Behold, the days come, saith the Lord, when I will make a new covenant with the house of Israel and with the house of Judah:9 Not according to the covenant that I made with their fathers in the day when I took them by the hand to lead them out of the land of Egypt; because they continued not in my covenant, and I regarded them not, saith the Lord. 10 For this is the covenant that I will make with the

---

[34] In other words, they learn to live the crucified life.

house of Israel after those days, saith the Lord; ***I will put my laws into their mind, and write them in their hearts:*** and I will be to them a God, and they shall be to me a people:

Now the heart has a change of focus from which to operate, namely, the Laws of God, which He wrote upon the heart. The New Covenant believer, however, must decide to yield to that new heart, living out their life within the desires of that new heart. If they decide to follow the things of God, they merely yield to the Holy Spirit's draw and resist the plans, schemes and pulls of the human heart. The power of the Holy Spirit within the believer assists and gives strength when making choices, however, the final decision to follow *"faith" (which holds hands with the new heart)*, or to follow the *"human heart" (which holds to its old ways)*, stays with the believer.

Faith's Goals:
As one walks with God, the main goal is to live a life on this earth, which pleases God. Faith, with its inherent leadership qualities, positions the believer to shift their focus on obtaining goals of eternal value, goals that God's Word readily defines. Thus, the Bible helps believers to acquire a cognitive perception of God's kingdom principles, His plans, and His purposes. Thus, living by "faith" makes God's kingdom's goals for humankind attainable.

To sum up some defining qualities of "faith":
- Faith, once received, opens the door to Salvation, helping to enter our rest.
- Faith walks hand in hand with the principle of rest.
- Faith builds the foundation of the believer's everyday life.
- Faith is the strong leader, a powerful champion, focusing the believer to obtain goals of God's kingdom with its eternal values.
- Faith exists and expresses itself to believers, giving believers an ability, once followed, to soar into the higher realms of living upon the earth.

A lifestyle of faith leads to complete fulfillment in every aspect of a person's life, producing what God deems best for each individual, and for all those whose lives touch those of the believer. It is no wonder *the just should live by faith!*

Words Make A Difference

This concept regarding the powerful influence of the human heart, originated back in the First Testament, and Yeshua, when He walked the earth, ensured His disciples knew about the heart and its ability to deceive, or as He put it, "defile a man".

Matthew 15:18
18 But those things which proceed out of the

mouth come forth from the heart; and they defile the man. 19 For out of the heart proceed evil thoughts, murders, adulteries, fornications, thefts, false witness, blasphemies:

Yeshua's teaching confirms that decisions come from the heart, showing an intricate connection between the "mouth" and the "heart". This speaks of "words", which intent stems from within the heart. Words are extremely important, and that importance escalates for a believer who walks by faith.

Remember, at the beginning of the "faith walk", believers *verbally speak* their choice to receive Salvation[35], and after salvation, they walk by "faith" as they make additional choices to serve the Lord in every circumstance of life. *Their words give direction to their individual life, declaring the focus and goals chosen by them, as they walk with the Lord.* It is imperative that all words spoken align with the direction in which God desires to take the believer. That way is always pursuant to the ways of righteousness, fulfilling His will and ensuring His kingdom's arrival in every situation.

If a person, after salvation, has difficulty in following the desires of the Holy Spirit, the problem shows up in everyday life manifesting in behaviour, and in words coming from the heart. It all goes back to Yeshua's

---

[35] Romans 10:8-10

teaching. If a person has learned to embrace the concepts of "faith", it will show in words and deeds. If they give "faith" the leadership role in all their heart, line up their speech and actions with that faith, they are well on their way to fulfilling the will of God in their lives.

How Does One Find Faith?
Paul, the Apostle tells us:

> Romans 10:17
> 17 So then faith comes by hearing, and hearing by the word of God.

It is imperative that new believers read the Bible to renew their mind. Then, once their renewed mind grasps the Word, believers speak that Word, learn its precepts, and employ the principles of God's kingdom in their lives.

In this manner, the believer trains themselves to think as God thinks. That was not a possibility under the First Covenant, but in the New Covenant since believers have the "mind of Messiah", God has equipped them to think like Yeshua[36]. If we learn to think like Yeshua, yielding to the indwelling power of the Holy Spirit, then the image we portray to others

---

[36] 1 Corinthians 2:16 For who hath known the mind of the Lord, that he may instruct him? But we have the mind of Christ.

will not be that of the fallen humankind, but rather that of the Second Adam, namely Yeshua. Through God's power and plans within the New Covenant salvation, expressing a positive image of God becomes a reality due to the power of the Holy Spirit and the yielded vessel of the believer. This is where the Holy Spirit desires to take each believer *if they agree to come along*.

In Summary

Since the "just shall live by faith", believers must grasp the necessity and reality of "faith". As we have seen, God made man to believe. Therefore, with His help and spiritual provisions prepared, believers receive opportunity to live in a greater connection with God than otherwise known before salvation.

Looking at the Hebrew word faith, we recognize that faith is a strong leader guiding us in every activity of life, in every circumstance. Once followed, faith, *which in itself is grounded or rooted in righteousness*, we walk in the paths of righteousness.

As believers, walking by faith, we learn to recognize, acknowledge, and yield to faith's leadership, choosing it over the leadership of the human heart. In other words, we die to self, to the wants of the heart. When we follow faith, we rest upon a solid foundation, upon which every aspect of life securely and firmly rests. Thus, reading, understanding, and speaking the Word of God, and at the same time, renewing the mind, we discover and then, embrace the ways of God.

Doing all of the above, *with the help of the Holy Spirit Who indwells the innermost being of the New Testament believer,* we set the stage to think, speak, act, and respond like God, thus showing His image to others upon the earth. Inadvertently, we also fulfill the individual purpose for which God gave us life.

The faith walk is a walk of rest, trusting in God's ways. Human thinking does not understand this, however, this where the rubber meets the road in the Christian experience.

Beloved, learn to shift gears to live by faith.
Determine to do things God's Way!

 ## Made to Align

"And there are three that bear witness in earth, the Spirit, and the water, and the blood: and these three agree in one".
1 John 5:8

Once we determine to exchange our heart's leadership for that of faith's leadership, we go through the door to a walk above the elementary things of the earth:

Galatians 4:9
"But now, after that ye have known God, or rather are known of God, how turn ye again to the weak and beggarly *(elementary)* elements, whereunto ye desire again to be in bondage?

When we learn to walk by faith, we align ourselves with the principles that God put in place, waiting to be ceased by God's people. Thus, through faith's leadership, we walk above and beyond the normal ways of mankind, ways where the human heart pulls us. In this stage of walking by faith we accept the opportunity to align, or agree with the principles of God, which bring the supernature things of God into the world in which we live. Aligning with God, in this manner, brings for the great fruit for the kingdom of God.

Walking in alignment with God, we walk hand-in-hand with Him, Who initiated our "faith walk", through the Word of salvation which He sent, and we received at the point of our new birth. From that point on, as we install "faith" as the foundation upon which we build our relationship and expression of our Christianity, we walk in our destined place with God.

To do that, we must earnestly take up the task of learning God's Word which enables us to think as God thinks. When we pick up the Bible, *authored by the Holy Spirit*, we pick up *"God's Instruction Manual on How to Live a Christian Life"*. With information in hand on how God's thinks, as we learned in an earlier chapter, we rid mindsets unacceptable to God and embrace those acceptable to Him.

Thinking in the same manner as God thinks becomes possible. Since New Covenant believers have the mind of Messiah [37] [38] this equips us to grasp the concepts of our new life and live it out.

---

[37] 1 Corinthians 2:16 For who hath known the mind of the Lord, that he may instruct him? But we have the mind of Christ.

In other words, dear reader, once believers learn the basic principles of New Covenant living, which God specified in His Word, believers then must give full consent to restructure their lives around God's principles, including His focus and goals for their new life in Him. Put plainly, once saved, we must go about the all-important task of learning God's Word, in order to discover His principles for New Testament living and learn to live by them.

As we familiarize ourselves with the source that speaks of God, the Bible, we open wide the appropriate door to know more of Him and how He designed us to live. Once we step inside that door with God, we unlock marvellous truths, which help us in our task of adjusting our lives according to His Word, including learning to ride above the base or elementary principles of this earth.

This kind of agreement or alignment with God, in most cases, requires a big attitude adjustment. That adjustment, as mentioned earlier, began at Salvation,

---

[38]. Isaiah 55:9 says, "For as the heavens are higher than the earth, so are my ways higher than your ways, and my thoughts than your thoughts". Under the First Covenant believers could not think like Messiah, but under the New Covenant, since the Holy Spirit dwells within, one can think like God. That does not mean you will know everything God knows. It means, you will function within the mindset of God, knowing His will, if not immediately, when God makes it known as you seek His Face.

and from then on, our thoughts must continue to follow a pathway leading us to perceive things God's way.

To see eye-to-eye with God requires embracing new concepts and, at the same time, disposing of others, those that do not produce a Godkind of fruit. This retraining begins at the new birth and continues as long as we have breath. However, a rule of thumb to follow, a guide to ensure all is in proper order is this:

Ensure our house, our body in which we dwell, matches the design of God's House.

Simply put, our old foundation which included principles and philosophies of this world, must be replaced. In its place, we must allow the new foundation of solid, faith principles learned from the Word of God to take root. In positioning each foundational block, *(each new principle we embrace)*, we align it with the cornerstone, Yeshua.

Since we are the building which God inhabits, we structure our new foundation and the life we build upon it, to His greater honour and glory. Therefore, as we weed out the world's influence, with its philosophies and values for living, we receive God's principles and viewpoints for living, no matter how contrary they seem to the world.

Paul, the Apostle, put it this way:

Ephesians 2:19-22
> 19 Now therefore ye are no more strangers and foreigners, but fellowcitizens with the saints, and of the household of God; 20 And are built upon the foundation of the apostles and prophets, Jesus Christ himself being the chief corner stone; 21 In whom all the building fitly framed together groweth unto an holy temple in the Lord: 22 In whom ye also are builded together for an habitation of God through the Spirit.

Paul, in teaching the Gentiles in the city of Ephesus, reminded those believers of their former days, when they were foreigners, living outside of God's household. Now, due to their acceptance of Yeshua, they belong to a new household, a new building.

These teachings of the Apostles and Prophets, with Yeshua as the cornerstone, comprise the foundation of that new building and thus, each person must personally see to it that their life aligns and embraces what God designed for them. Upon that solid, God-ordained structure or foundation, each believer sits and once positioned, form the remainder of the building, which Paul labels God's holy house or temple, the place of His habitation by the Holy Spirit.

Instead of operating their lives from a former pagan mindset which modeled their foundation, these Gentile believers must put those former teachings aside to accept the teachings of the Apostles and Prophets. This meant abandoning their old foundation, one in which God never dwelt. They now must accept the fact that they are a prepared vessel, a Holy Habitation, in which a holy and pure God resides.

Gentile believers, in the early church struggled, however, they tried to embrace a new foundation, discarding the old, world system to align with God's kingdom principles. These Gentiles of whom Paul speaks, were not alone in the challenge of rebuilding their faith foundation. Jewish converts to Christianity also faced many challenges arising from their former foundation of faith.

While Jews perhaps knew the principle to "live by faith", their faith practices in feasts, sacrifices and rituals needed to reflect the New Covenant and hence their earlier practices must adjust. Now, their long-awaited Messiah, once foreshadowed in their earlier faith practices, came and with His coming, the old system of worship ended. Their former sacrificial system, once prophetically demonstrating Yeshua's coming, must reflect the fulfillment that Yeshua's coming brought.

In addition, the Torah had a slightly different place within the New Covenant of Grace[39]. Paul taught the Jews, that the Torah[40] existed for the purposes of showing sin's existence but once aware of sin, the *prophetic aspect of the sacrificial system* ended. In his letter to believers at Galatia, who struggled where to place the Torah in their thinking, Paul wrote:

Galatians 3:22-26
22 But the scripture has concluded all under sin, that the promise by faith of Jesus Christ might be given to them that believe. 23 But before faith came, we were kept under the law, shut up unto the faith which should afterwards be revealed. *24 Wherefore the law was our schoolmaster to bring us unto Christ, that we might be justified by faith.* 25 But after that faith is come, we are no longer under a schoolmaster. 26 For you are all the children of God by faith in Christ Jesus.

Once the Torah pointed out the need for Messiah, and with their acceptance of Him, they became justified, the purpose of that Torah changed because its assignment in that regard saw its fulfillment in their life. *Before salvation,* it was a schoolmaster but *after salvation,* at which point they were justified by faith, its role

---

[39] The terms, "New Covenant" & New Covenant of Grace are synonymous

[40] Torah means Instructions of God. (It is often interpreted as law, but this is not the best translation for that word).

changed. Many Jewish converts to Messianic Judaism were unprepared for that thinking and thus, faced a difficult challenge of adjusting their thinking in many aspects within the Torah. Many refused to do so and instead, they married the Torah to Grace and lived that way. To those, Paul wrote:

Galatians 5:1-7
> 1 Stand fast therefore in the liberty wherewith Christ hath made us free, and be not entangled again with the yoke of bondage. 2 Behold, I Paul say unto you, that if ye be circumcised, Christ shall profit you nothing. 3 For I testify again to every man that is circumcised, that he is a debtor to do the whole law. 4 Christ is become of no effect unto you, whosoever of you are justified by the law; *ye are fallen from grace.* 5 For we through the Spirit wait for the hope of righteousness by faith. 6 For in Jesus Christ neither circumcision availeth any thing, nor uncircumcision; but faith which worketh by love. 7 Ye did run well; *who did hinder you that ye should not obey the truth?*

New Covenant believers, saved by grace. et who chose to embrace circumcision as a means of salvation, according to Paul's words, fell from grace. Those that taught them to insist salvation came through circumcision and not by faith hindered them from obeying the truth.

To cut a long story of early church history short, all believers in Messiah, both Jew and Gentile, faced the task of incorporating a new foundation based on the New Covenant. Failure to do so meant that the faith dynamics, found within the Covenant of Grace, would fall by the wayside, unfulfilled. Only a new foundation, reflecting what God implemented with the establishment of the New Covenant, could position the believer for their new life in Messiah. When installed, this new foundation enabled them to live a triumphant life within Messiah, walking by faith, within the dynamics God made possible. [41]

As it was true in the first century Church, it is true today. Believers still come to salvation from diverse environments, some Jew, and some Gentile. Upon salvation, if these believers do not understand the need for a new foundation, they may well refuse the release their old foundation and try to live it out based on former mindsets, many that seem biblical in their eyes. Unknown to these believers, dormant and hidden in the recesses of their being, lurked snares, and robbers of "carnal" and "manmade" teachings, which came

---

[41] Later, in other chapters, you will find those dynamics explained in detail.

alive to influence their new faith, eventually damaging or shipwrecking it.

Old criteria deposited from former teachings strangle new life. The precious seed of faith God deposited, lands then, not in ground within the heart, where it should bud into maturity well rooted to stand a long time, but rather it falls elsewhere resulting in an unfulfilled Christian life.

When such happens to individuals, instead of looking at the old foundation as the problem, many blame Christianity, calling it inadequate, antiquated or even non-realistic. The solution to that dilemma is not to avoid, omit or discard Christianity, which some do, when they think its principles seem invalid.

Rather, one should look at the foundation on which they base their experience, to determine if it, first, agrees with God, and secondly, to see if it functions as God designed. If not, looking at the error, upon which the believer built his foundation, resolves the issue. This is a better way than pointing a finger at the God, Who gave the New Covenant in His own Son's blood.

God made us to align with Him. That alignment to His Ways, however, lays in our hands. We must choose to do so.

Accepting The New Foundation

In order to keep things functioning well, as God intended, let us accept the idea of a new foundation, and then, let us use faith's principles and put it in place.

Romans 12:1-2
> 1 I beseech you therefore, brethren, by the mercies of God, that ye present your bodies a living sacrifice, holy, acceptable unto God, which is your reasonable service. 2 And be not conformed to this world: but be ye transformed *by the renewing of your mind*, that ye may prove what is that good, and acceptable, and perfect, will of Go.

Here the Apostle Paul's advice is clear and specific. Renew your mind. Do not conform to the world and its thinking, he warns. Present your bodies a living sacrifice, holy and acceptable to God.

Paul understood this faith walk required much discipline for Christian living and thus his admonition, to become a living sacrifice, embraced the idea of a personal sacrifice, which believers give to God. Paul compared the experience of changing mindsets to a sacrifice placed in the fires of the altar. Old thinking, firmly rooted in a foundation which self embraced, does not die easily *unless self dies* too. That self-death is painful.

Believers who wish to pursue God, choosing to do only that which pleases Him, face an extraction of all self based activities and goals. These must receive a deathblow; otherwise, these detract from a total surrender to the Living God. Such blows are not too welcomed as often *the flesh* in humanity, as it dies, complains with agonizing pain.

Flesh's first instinct declines God's principles, especially when it touches self, self's accompaniments and its goals. When self must die due to agreement with Holy Spirit's leading, *unless the person is 100% resolved to serve the Lord*, struggles occur. Lack of resolution and determination in this matter produces greater struggles.

Nevertheless, this is the call. This is the faith walk. This is the sacrifice required. The sooner believers decide to renew their minds and shift their entire life into full gear to live in "agreement with God", the sooner believers release their old ways, demolish the old foundation, and set about building the new one. Once the surrender takes place, however, the thinking, *once adjusted to God's ways*, brings about a wonderful, fulfilling relationship with God, the fruit of which satisfies to the depth of the inner most being.

In the beginning, after we first hear the call to change, we face a rather large challenge. We must discard former faulty foundations, *in faith,* that God requires it. For the new believer, who knows not *experientially* the rewards of the relationship, they must, nevertheless, pay the required price upon that sacrificial altar trusting and believing that what God requires of them is, in the end, the best for them. The choice is not easy; however, the Holy Spirit stands ready to help and to give strength for a complete resolve, which refuses any option to change one's mind.

Make The Decision
Regarding the foundation on which you base your life, dear reader, remember, each believer decides whether to remove the old foundation and embrace the new, or not. Each believer makes the decision to yield to the "new heart" received at conversion or follow the old one. The starting point is your cognitive surrender, to do things God's way, to agree with Him, what He says, does, and desires, consenting to the fact that He knows best.

It sounds so simple to say it but living it out requires strong perseverance and rust in God. The process from Salvation to the completely revamped Christian life aligned with God in all things, takes time. It takes prayer, determination, and dedication, not to mention that it cannot happen without the power of the Holy Spirit. Such change includes an understanding that we serve a God Who is holy, set apart from the world with all its lusts and lures. It follows that, if we are to present His image on the earth, we must practise His same behaviour. Whatsoever we formerly established, to keep "self" happy, is the first to go into the fires on the sacrificial altar. Daily, one situation at a time, crucifying self and yielding to a holy life, presents the characteristics of a normal crucifixion, a slow and painful death. To quote the Apostle Paul, "I die daily".[42]

As reinforced throughout this chapter, our decision to make Messiah Lord in our own personal life necessitates embracing the concept to change former mindsets, to accept Him and His Ways, and, at the same time, step away from our own. Many think that salvation is all that God requires. Those with that concept may not have heard the call to embrace a life where self dies. They might see Salvation as only a new beginning, and that it is, a beginning! As far as a walk with God goes, it emphatically means the end to a self life. After Salvation becomes a reality, it becomes the believer's turn to die. This is what Yeshua said, so long ago to His disciples:

Matthew 16:24-25
   24 Then said Jesus unto his disciples, *If any man will come after me, let him deny himself, and take up his cross, and follow me.* 25 For whosoever will save his

---
[42] 1 Corinthians 15:31

life shall lose it: and whosoever will lose his life for my sake shall find it.

To "save one's life" is to choose *not* to die to self, not to present your life upon that sacrificial altar, mentioned in Romans 12. It is to allow self to rule, which in turn, rises up to overrule the new heart given at Salvation. To lose one's life for Messiah's sake means complete, unreserved surrender, of one's entire being, delivering it into the Hands of the Living God for such purposes as He wills.

The Apostle Paul, in speaking of a surrendered life related to the Galatians:

Galatians 2:20
20 "I am crucified with Christ: nevertheless, I live; yet not I, but Christ lives in me: and the life which I now live in the flesh I live by the faith of the Son of God, who loved me, and gave himself for me".

In Paul's words, the principle of living by "faith" appears as paramount in his life. It shows that instead of Paul living his own life, Messiah lives *in the crucified vessel*, or perhaps more accurately, *through it*. This kind of life produces aspects of God's character in the believer, which is a good fruit. Great surrender produces great fruit, which, in God's viewpoint, far outweighs the costs.

Messiah, living through Paul, did not make him a robot, nor will He do so to today's believers. Paul's admonition to live by faith, dying to self, rather gives another message.

Paul's life relays a prescription for living the Christian life, wherein the whole body, mind, soul, and spirit functions in the way God intended.

Such living culminates in a close, endearing, and enduring relationship with the Almighty. Such vessels change the world by Him, through Him and for Him. This is the true promise of the Christian life. Its costs are many and so are its rewards, which, by the way, are *not temporal*, fading away into obscurity. Rewards for true Christian living, satisfies the longing of the soul, in this life, and goes on to an eternity filled with God and eternal rewards. However, these ends come only by taking up the cross, which means denying oneself just as Yeshua said. To those who wished to follow Him,[43] the path leads directly towards the cross, the place of death!

Perhaps, when you heard the gospel message, you heard it differently. Some preachers like to whitewash the gospel message when they offer Salvation, speaking only of the cost Yeshua paid, without speaking of the cost one pays to live their life as God's

---

[43] Matthew 16:24

adopted son or daughter. If Yeshua found His mission's completion at the cross and later received the glory, His seed, (which includes all believers), must find the same thing. As the expression says, "the cross comes before the crown".[44]

<u>In Summary:</u>
Agreement with God begins at Salvation and continues throughout the believer's life. To understand how to agree with God, believers must gain a working knowledge of God's Word, and so, learning the Word is the first order of business after Salvation. Once we have the information as God presented in His Word, we then make a choice whether to follow it or keep our own ways.

When we choose to agree with God, we chose to adjust our foundation. As we do, we begin the disassembling of our old foundation, *(which, by the way, aligned with the "heart" we possessed prior to our conversion),* and then, agreeing with God's principles of faith within the New Covenant, we construct the new foundation, *(which aligns with the new heart given at Salvation).*

As we employ the reconstructive process of our life, we adjust in our thinking, thus renewing our minds to align with biblical, New Covenant principles of Grace

---

[44] This saying means, the rewards, symbolized by the crown, do not come before the challenge, symbolized by the cross.

and life in Messiah. In summary, we see that "self dies" and the "seed of life deposited by God", lives. Having taken whatever measures necessary to learn how God thinks, we revamp our former mindsets, exchanging them for new mindsets that agree with God. Beloved, consider the eternal value of things!

Chose to die to self and live to God in a life of faith! You were made to align with God. Do so and you will find that it is well worth the price you paid!

COURSE 204

SECTION 2

MOLDED FOR GOD'S GOVERNMENT

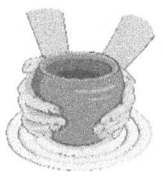 **Made to Live**

"Where is boasting then? It is excluded. By what law? of works? Nay: but by the law of faith".

Romans 3:27

Thus far, Molded for the Miraculous" stressed the importance of walking by faith, showing the reader that God made us in His image, and after the fall, enabled us, through salvation's open door, to watch, rest, believe and align with Him. However, we have not yet entwined those thoughts with the purpose of humankind upon the earth, other than to see how these aspects of the Christian life work towards the ultimate goal of expressing God's image in the believer. Before we can return to the theme of "watching over the earth" to show how it is possible to fulfil humankind's original purpose, we must take another sidestep.

This sidestep helps us to understand *two unique laws* upon the earth. These two laws, like the Law of Gravity, operate upon the earth, whether we know it or not. In this chapter, we will look at the first law, the one that automatically affects human life upon the earth. In the next chapter, we will look at the other law which comes only by a definite and clear choice.

To understand this first law, *that law by which all humankind are subjected,* we must review a little. In an earlier Chapter of this book, you read Genesis 1:26-28 wherein God gave humankind "dominion" over the fish of the sea, the fowls of the air, the cattle, and over all the earth, including every living creature that crawled upon it.

When looking at the word "dominion", in its original Hebrew picture language, we saw that it depicted **Adam's authoritative rulership** over all the doorways of the earth, showing God's clear intentions that *whatever situations or circumstances Adam encountered, God designed him to be victorious.* God's decision, to release that assignment to Adam, positioned Adam, his wife, and descendants, to govern the earth. Summed up then, in what is often called Adam's commission, God ordained Adam to walk in dominion upon the earth, governing it responsibly as God Himself would govern it.

Unfortunately, as we saw earlier, Adam disobeyed God in the Garden of Eden.

While Adam had the ability to assert God's will and thus govern in alignment with God's kingdom, Adam chose not to do so. As a result, Adam's government mantled to "rule" and "subdue" fled away as a direct consequence of his choice not to keep earth in alignment with God's kingdom. Adam, his wife, and their seed (their children) became subject to "sin and death". This sin and death became a new law which governed the earth in Adam's place.

Paul, the apostle, called that new governing authority, "the Law of Sin and Death.

The Law of Sin and Death

>Romans 8:2
>>2 For the law of the Spirit of life in Christ Jesus hath made me free *from the law of sin and death*

In Paul's dissertation to the Romans, he identified the law which came into effect after Adam failed to govern in alignment with God's kingdom, and he named a new law that God brought in through Yeshua. He spoke of two major laws:

1. The Law of the Spirit of Life
2. The Law of Sin and Death

When we understand the Law of Sin and Death, we can better grasp the Law of the Spirit of Life. So, let us get started learning about the Law of Sin and Death.

First, the Law of sin and death came upon all mankind automatically, by Adam's choice. The Apostle Paul put it this way:

> Romans 5:12
> "Wherefore, as by one man sin entered into the world, and death by sin; and so, death passed upon all men, for that all have sinned:"

Clearly, Adam sinned; death entered the world; and from then on, every person dwelling upon the earth, meets face to face with death at their life's end. That is the basic message in the first Adam as Paul related it to those in Rome.

The Characteristics of Sin and Death

Once sin entered the world, other things resulted in the earth such as pain, sorrow, and grief. Also, parts of the body experienced a type of death, where things, at times, cease to function properly. We call that sickness, disease, and infirmities. All of these things operate in our world, which we call "fallen", as a direct result of sin's entrance. These effects of Sin and Death, which originate from the power of Darkness, remember, are not ***God's perfect plan*** for humankind.

There is a world of difference between the power of Darkness and God's kingdom, which we can also call, the Kingdom of Light. In the interests of gaining a better understanding about the two laws Paul spoke of, the Law of Sin and Death, and the Law of the Spirit of Life, let us compare the two sources of these laws. [45]

<u>The Power of Darkness</u>
Death, along with sickness, disease and the like, originated from darkness. Of course, do not forget, activities of "sin" derive from that place, too! Whenever people agree to align with "sin", they follow the desires of the flesh. Paul, the Apostle, describes some of these works of the flesh.

Galatians 5:19-21
> 19 Now the works of the flesh are manifest, which are [these]; Adultery, fornication, uncleanness, lasciviousness, 20 Idolatry, witchcraft, hatred, variance, emulations, wrath, strife, seditions, heresies, 21 Envyings, murders, drunkenness, revellings, and such like: of the which I tell you before, as I have also told [you] in time past, that they which do such things shall not inherit the kingdom of God.

---

[45] Please keep in mind, there really is no comparison between the power of darkness and the kingdom of God, however, the comparison contrasts one with the other to help grasp their concepts.

People practising these works of the flesh, as Paul calls them, do not always recognize the source of the deed is *the flesh, nor its influence* by the power of Darkness. Without knowing it, people invite many harmful influences into their lives, most of which come upon them unexpectedly. For example, carnal sins, which foster various addictions, keep the person bound to express that snare and the sin which results from it. No matter how hard they struggle, they cannot free themselves. This connection, which comes from the power of Darkness, must break, *first*, before the person enjoys complete freedom.

While God's code of behaviour for humankind, the 10 commandments, identifies what He defines as sin, and at the same time, shows mankind's need for a Saviour, many people still do not grasp the idea of being trapped by the power of darkness, and in need of a way of escape. Scripture teaches this happens because of a "blindness" which sin brings with it. In other words, people trapped in sin, cannot see the trap, nor the way out. Many think "this is life" and struggle independent from God's help.

Part of Yeshua's mission upon the earth, as declared by His own mouth, was to "open the eyes of the blind":

> Luke 4:18
> 18 The Spirit of the Lord is upon me, because he hath anointed me to preach the gospel to the poor;

he hath sent me to heal the brokenhearted, to preach deliverance to the captives, and *recovering of sight to the blind,* to set at liberty them that are bruised,

Additional parts of Yeshua's mission include preaching, which carries God's passionate message of deliverance to the ears of the poor in spirit, held captive by sin. That amazing message includes God's desire and ability to heal the brokenhearted, free the captives, give sight to the blind, and give freedom to the bruised or injured in this life.

Before God's supernatural Hand moves into action, however, first, the person hears God's compassionate message, and through that message recognizes God's love and His solution their problem. To put it another way, first people need to see their sin and its results, before they seek a solution, which, once they hear are free to accept or reject.

On that same theme, Luke, in the book of Acts, records Yeshua's words as He commissioned the Apostle Paul to preach the gospel:

Acts 26:15-18
15 And I said, Who are you, Lord? And he said, I am Yeshua, whom you persecute. 16 But rise, and stand upon your feet: for I have appeared

unto you for this purpose, to make you a minister and a witness both of these things which you have seen, and of those things in the which I will appear unto you; 17 Delivering you from the people, and from the Gentiles, unto whom now I send you, 18 *To open their eyes, and to turn them from darkness to light, and from the power of Satan unto God, that they may receive forgiveness of sins, and inheritance among them which are sanctified by faith that is in me.*

Those caught in sin's trap are surely blind to the trap, and also how to be free. Furthermore, the Bible calls these individuals snared in sin's trap as prisoners. King David knew this and related both the dilemma and the solution in the following Psalm:

Psalms 107:8-20
8 Oh that men would praise YeHoVaH for his goodness, and for his wonderful works to the children of men! 9 For he satisfies the longing soul and fills the hungry soul with goodness. *10 Such as sit in darkness and in the shadow of death, being bound in affliction and iron;* 11 Because they rebelled against the words of God and contemned[46] the counsel of the most High: 12 Therefore he brought down their heart with labour; they fell down, and there was none to

---
[46] Spurned

help. 13 Then they cried unto YeHoVaH in their trouble, and he saved them out of their distresses. *14 He brought them out of darkness and the shadow of death and brake their bands in sunder.* 15 Oh that men would praise YeHoVaH for his goodness, and for his wonderful works to the children of men! *16 For he has broken the gates of brass and cut the bars of iron in sunder.* 17 Fools because of their transgression, and because of their iniquities, are afflicted. 18 Their soul abhors all manner of meat; and *they draw near unto the gates of death.* 19 Then they cry unto YeHoVaH in their trouble, and he saves them out of their distresses. *20 He sent his word, and healed them, and delivered them from their destructions.*

While there are many prophetic indications of Yeshua in this Psalm, the imagery speaks clearly of each living person as a prisoner to darkness and death, held in its grasp with strong restraints, all of which God breaks when humankind recognizes the problem and seeks God's help. Thus, escape from the power of Darkness, is possible for all those who "see" the need and "receive" the solution.

The Kingdom of Light
This, obviously, speaks of God's kingdom. It is the place from which all life stems, including eternal life.

Many scriptures speak of some qualities of the Kingdom of Light, so below you will find a chart with scriptures, and then a recapped column showing the benefit mentioned[47] when God's kingdom comes.[48]

Benefits Of God's Kingdom	
Scripture	Characteristic
Isaiah 35: 5 Then the eyes of the blind shall be opened, and the ears of the deaf shall be unstopped.	• Blind eyes open • Deaf ears open
Psalm 146:8 YeHoVaH opens [the eyes of] the blind: YeHoVaH raises them that are bowed down: YeHoVaH loves the righteous:	• Blind eyes open • Bowed down raised up
Matthew 11:5 The blind receive their sight, and the lame walk, the lepers are cleansed, and the deaf hear, the dead are raised up, and the poor have the gospel preached to them.	• Blind receive sight • Lame walk • Lepers cleansed (healed) • Dead raised up • Poor hear gospel

---

[47] Some scriptures repeat certain benefits. Note how many times it mentions that "blind eyes" are opened.
[48] These benefits, which are available to us, come when the Lord brings His Kingdom to touch our lives, in one way or another.

Luke 24:45 Then opened he their understanding, that they might understand the scriptures,	• Understanding of scripture opened
Acts 26:18 To open their eyes, [and] to turn [them] from darkness to light, and [from] the power of ha satan unto God, that they may receive forgiveness of sins, and inheritance among them which are sanctified by faith that is in me.	• Open eyes • Turn them (away) from darkness • Turn them (toward) light • Turn them (away) from the power of ha satan, (the adversary) • Turn them (toward) the power of God • Forgiveness of sin to all sanctified by faith in Yeshua (remember, the Just shall live by faith!)
2 Corinthians 4:6 For God, who commanded the light to shine out of darkness, hath shined in our hearts, to [give] the light of the knowledge of the glory of God in the face of Jesus Christ.	• God commands light to shine out of darkness • It shines into hearts • It gives them the light of knowledge of Yeshua, Who is God's glory
Isaiah 9:2 The people that walked in darkness have	• People walking in darkness see a great

seen a great light: they that dwell in the land of the shadow of death, upon them hath the light shined.	light • Those dwelling in the land of the shadow of death, have light upon them

Many more scriptures tell us about God's kingdom. These few, however, convey the main idea, especially regarding the Law of Sin and Death. It is from that law *that God frees humankind* when they seek His Face. He opens their eyes so they may see their sin, see the bondage they live in, and praise the Lord, see the way out through Yeshua, Ha' Maschiach!

This message of Scripture clearly shows us that God does not desire for mankind to live beneath the Law of Sin and Death. No! He wanted humankind to rise about the Law of Sin and Death. In short, God wanted humankind to live! Life was God's plan for humankind, unfortunately, humankind through Adam, the first man, chose death.

Remember that God created mankind sufficient to stand but free to fall. So, once mankind fell, God opened a door to ensure they could find restoration in Him. In that restoration, He gave mankind a way to live, and to rise above the very thing which strove to take them down, namely death. That door He opened to all humankind was salvation through Yeshua! Thus, with compassion, love, and mercy, from Adam until

Yeshua's second coming, God cries out to all who will hear Him, "Be saved". In other words, God calls all humankind to live:

Deuteronomy 30:19
> 19 I call heaven and earth to record this day against you, [that] I have set before you life and death, blessing and cursing: therefore, choose life, that both thou and thy seed may live:

Then, from mankind's individual redemption's cry to His ears, His Spirit responds by releasing eternal life. With eternal life now given to humankind, God positions all in Yeshua to arise! This aspect we see in the next chapter.

In Summary
1. Every person born upon this earth is subject to the Law of Sin and Death. This effect came upon all humankind after Adam sinned.
2. Every person from Adam yields to sin and thus becomes bound to that sin and its effects, and although you cannot physically see it, wear chains from the power of Darkness, from which they cannot be free on their own.

On this same note, the bible tells us "The soul that sins, shall die".[49] Thus, every person born upon the earth will die, first because of the "death sentence" inherited from Adam and secondly due to the merit of their own choices to sin. The only escape is the provision God made for all humankind, namely that of Yeshua.

Although this book did not discuss this, the basic tenants of the Christian faith declare that:
- Yeshua was born of the seed of *a woman*, and thus did not inherit the "death sentence from Adam"
- Yeshua never sinned, not even once in any area of His life. He pleased God always.

No other person, who walked upon this earth, ever lived 100% perfectly in God's eyes. Yeshua alone did so, and through His perfect obedience to God, made it possible for all those who choose Him as Saviour, to be free from the chains of sin and its consequences, including death. Thus, when one chooses Yeshua, one is born-again, but this time, born of the Holy Spirit, Who now dwells within the believer. Thus, the person, in God's eyes, are positioned above the Law of Sin and Death, called to arise.

While a person, in their human flesh dies, God promises a resurrection body, and also, eternal life so

---

[49] Ezekiel 18:20

death does not have an eternal power over them. Rather, those born again, those in Messiah, now become subject to a new law: The Law of the Spirit of Life, which subject is discussed in the next chapter.

Beloved, if you are born again, be encouraged.
With the power of the Holy Spirit living in you, and God's promise of eternal life,
you no longer need to fear death!
With God's help, you arise to your greater destiny!

 **Made to Arise**

"But if the Spirit of him that raised up Jesus from the dead dwell in you, he that raised up Christ from the dead shall also quicken your mortal bodies by his Spirit that dwelleth in you".

Romans 8:11

In the last chapter, we saw that through Adam's choice, his seed inherited the Law of Sin and Death. While there is no escape from that Law, God, in His great Mercy, *implemented another Law* which gives humanity a way out. That Law only comes into effect when a human being makes the decision to accept Yeshua as Saviour. When that decision is heartfelt and genuine, God implements a new Law in the life of the saved person. *That Law operates by Faith*, as does all other Laws within the Kingdom of God.

All saved people, according to the Apostle Paul, can now to live by a different law, having been freed from the Law of Sin and Death".

Romans 8:2

2 For *the law of the Spirit of life in Christ Jesus* hath

made me free from the law of sin and death

This Law, the first one named in Romans 8, is the Law which comes *only by choice* through accepting God's plan of salvation.

The Law of The Spirit of Life:
Those who made the decision to receive God's gift of Salvation, must learn to operate within the Law of the Spirit of Life. It is a vastly different Law than the Law of Sin and Death. First, it is a superior law in that it operates by God's Holy Spirit. Immediately upon Salvation, God initiates this Law, bringing about an amazing change within the believer's spirit. Believers now have "Life" where before they had "death". Secondly, the difference shows in the operation of that law. To receive the full effect or impact of that law depends *on further choices*, which of course, depends on grasping, *by faith the workings of that new law.*

According to the Apostle Paul, in his letter to the Colossians, once redemption comes to us, we are no *longer subjects* of the power of Darkness. He said,

Colossians 1:9-13
> 9 For this cause we also, since the day we heard it, do not cease to pray for you, and to desire that you might be filled with the knowledge of his will in all wisdom and spiritual understanding; 10 That you

might walk worthy of the Lord unto all pleasing, being fruitful in every good work, and increasing in the knowledge of God; 11 Strengthened with all might, according to his glorious power, unto all patience and longsuffering with joyfulness; 12 Giving thanks unto the Father, which hath made us meet to be partakers of the inheritance of the saints in light: **13 Who hath delivered us from the power of darkness**

Since we are "translated" from the power of darkness, into God's kingdom, we now have opportunity to learn new laws: the laws of the Kingdom of God. Since the new Kingdom is God's own Kingdom, or the Kingdom of Light, the principles or Laws of that kingdom govern our lives. Again, we must align or agree wit these laws, since they operate based on faith. First, we learn the principles and then, learn how to appropriate them.

Translated Into God's Kingdom

This word in Colossians 1:13 interpreted by KJV as "translated" comes from the Greek word, μεθιστημι (meth-is'-tay-mee). There are two root words found in this word, one meaning "established" and the other meaning "afterward", or "elsewhere". Summarized, the word means, *established elsewhere*. There is a picture here, then, of leaving one place and arriving elsewhere.

A good example of the meaning of this word shows up in the book of Acts, as it speaks of an incident in the life of Apostle Philip

> Acts 8:38-40
> 38 And he commanded the chariot to stand still: and they went down both into the water, both Philip and the eunuch; and he baptized him. *39 And when they were come up out of the water, the Spirit of the Lord caught away Philip, that the eunuch saw him no more*: and he wen. on his way rejoicing. 40 But **Philip was found at Azotus:** and passing through he preached in all the cities, till he came to Caesarea.

Philip, once alongside the Ethiopian eunuch, suddenly disappeared out of the eunuch's sight. The Holy Spirit carried Philip to another place, named Azotus. Clearly, Philip left one place and showed up in another. The action, whereby the Holy Spirit carried Philip, we call "translation". When understanding the meaning of "translated into the Kingdom of his dear Son",[50] we keep in mind the concept of leaving one place for another.

When one is born-again, the Holy Spirit, through His amazing ability, removes the believer from the power of darkness, which, of course, originates in the "power

---

[50] Colossians 1:13

of Darkness". Keep in mind, whether human beings know it or not, the unsaved live supressed or beneath this power, influenced by it, and before salvation, are hopelessly chained to it. At Salvation, the Holy Spirit breaks the chains holding them to the power of Darkness and sets them free, and then places the believer inside the Kingdom of God. Now the believer has opportunity to function under the laws of God's kingdom, for God made the believer to arise above the other Law of Sin and Death!

Remember, this experience of "translation", which happens to every believer, makes it possible for believers to live within the principles of the kingdom of God, being that *they are now part of that kingdom*. Again, the principles within the Kingdom of God operate by faith, thus as believers change former mindsets and embrace new ones, the believer functions within their new environment. That new environment is neither visually seen by believers, nor felt. Most do not understand the silent and hidden miracle, or its honoured privileges, that God granted them at Salvation. In God's eyes, every believer is part of His Kingdom, and an intricate part of His Son, Yeshua.

On that same topic, Paul, the Apostle, explains the new life in Messiah in his dissertation to believers in Rome. As you read the scripture below, keep in mind, the Holy Spirit performs this action every time someone comes to Salvation. He can do so because, as deity, He is bound to neither time nor place.

Romans 6:3-7
> 3 Know you not, that so many of us as were baptized into Jesus Christ were baptized into his death? 4 Therefore we are buried with him by baptism into death: that like as Christ was raised up from the dead by the glory of the Father, even so we also should walk in newness of life. 5 For if we have been planted together in the likeness of his death, we shall be also in the likeness of his resurrection: 6 Knowing this, that our old man is crucified with him, so that the body of sin might be destroyed, that henceforth we should not serve sin. 7 For he that is dead is freed from sin.

This scripture does not speak of water baptism, although water baptism symbolizes its principles, but this scripture speaks of a miracle that God performs for every born-again believer. The Holy Spirit immerses, positions, or in Paul's words, baptizes the born-again believer, inside Yeshua. He places them into Yeshua's death on the cross and then, into the actual burial of Yeshua. Not wishing to leave them under the influences of death, He then immerses them into Yeshua's resurrection whereby believers arise In Yeshua and then, partake of new life. This experience happens by the Holy Spirit's power instantly upon salvation. It happens in order to bring the believer into both **the Redemptive** work of the cross, *which broke the power and consequences of sin, removing them from under the Law of Sin and Death,* and **the Resurrection**, *which brings about a believer's new life whereby they are subject to the Law of the Spirit of Life.*

When speaking of the baptism into Messiah's death, in Paul's words, "the old humankind is crucified". This phrase refers to the life the person lived formerly, when unsaved[51]. The "body of sin", by Holy Spirit power, is destroyed, (shattered, cracked, broken into small pieces), and thus, the person is no longer imprisoned to "sin". Thus, the bondage to the Law of Sin and Death breaks away, and the person is now "free" to live for God.

Now, translated from the power of darkness into the Kingdom of Light, (the Kingdom of God's dear Son), the believer lives with new goals, new focuses, and new behaviours, through the power of the Holy Spirit. In other words, the Holy Spirit translated the believer from darkness and its control to God's kingdom, freeing them from the Law of Sin and Death and making applicable in their life, the Law of the Spirit of Life. He also dwells within the believer and daily, as they desire to walk in God's ways, the Holy Spirit

---

[51] The phrase "old man", today, is a slang expression meaning someone's father. In no way does today's meaning apply.

produces the fruit of His Presence. We call that fruit, the "fruit of the Spirit".

Galatians 5:22-25
> 22 But the fruit of the Spirit is love, joy, peace, longsuffering, gentleness, goodness, faith, 23 Meekness, temperance: against such there is no law. 24 And they that are Christ's have crucified the flesh with the affections and lusts. 25 If we live in the Spirit, let us also walk in the Spirit.

Having understood that God translates the believer into His Kingdom, and thus, frees the believer from the power of darkness, we can now look at another Greek word in Colossians 1:13, which give us even more insight to this scripture:

Colossians 1:13
> 13 Who has delivered us from the power of darkness, and has translated us into the kingdom of his dear Son:

The phrase, "Who has delivered us from the power of darkness", looking at the word, "power" in the Greek, is what we will consider here. To us, the word for power usually means energy, strength, or control, but the Greek word used here gives us more insight. In Greek, the word εξουσια (ex-oo-see'-ah) carries with it the idea of decisions made by legal authorities. It is the judicial deciding ability of the power of darkness, which Paul refers to in Colossians 1:13. So to put it in modern terms, Colossians 1:13 says, in reference to the Father, He made us partakers in the inheritance of the saints, delivering us from the "legal, judicial, deciding ability" of the power of darkness. That puts a wider scope of understanding as to the meaning here. The power of Darkness, which could make decisions, with legal authority to do so on its victims, can no longer make decisions over believers. Why? Believers no longer are victims of the power of darkness! They are taken away and made citizens of a new kingdom, the Kingdom of God.

To further your understanding, dear reader, let me give you an example. Let us say you are born in a foreign land under the rulership of a cruel and harsh dictator. The laws within that land forced its citizens to live in great poverty. The government rules that its citizens must work hard, but every penny earned they take away with exorbitant tax laws. Your life is bitter and cruel.

Due to a miracle, you escape this land for a democracy. Upon your arrival, the government gives you set up monies to own property and an income to help you feed your family for a time until you find a job. You soon get that job and before you know it, you have saved a rather large sum of money in the bank. One day, your former government sends you a letter demanding you sell all you own and forward them the money. They threaten your life and that of your family if you do not cooperate.

Legally, the former government has no authority to operate within the new land where you immigrated. Their rulings do not legally apply to your life in your new homeland. You moved out of their jurisdiction and now live beyond their legislation. Thus, you are not obligated to obey their laws. *Your obligations are for the new government in the place where you now reside.* In short, your new government, that of a democracy, protects you from the laws of that horrible dictator. You, therefore, can ignore the threats and throw off the demands of that former government in the country you formerly resided.

Beloved, ask the Lord to help you get this important principle in your understanding. By order of God's proclamation or judgment, for the remainder of your life upon the earth, *the former judicial legislation of the power of Darkness* has *no legal right* to send rulings into your life. Yeshua removed it and upon your Salvation, the Holy Spirit removed you from the effects of that power. Darkness cannot *legally* make decisions over your life. You now belong to God. You live in His Kingdom. *Now His Laws apply to your life.* You only need to understand those laws, and then *apply them* to live your Christian life so you can live in victory!

Paul's letter to the Colossians makes it very clear that darkness has *no legal right* to make rulings, of any kind, in the life of a believer. *However, the power of Darkness, like the dictator in the example above, continues to send out laws and edicts over your life.* If you do not understand that God removed you from its judicial authority, then you will continue to accept its rulings and laws as applicable to your life. Thus, you will continue living in bondage to sin, sickness, grief, and the list of endless things, which originate from the power of Darkness. *If there is one place in which to immediately renew your mind after salvation, it is in this area.* Accept the fact of your translation from the power of darkness, into the Kingdom of God's Dear Son and live that way! *See yourself under the laws of a new government, that of the Kingdom of God!*

About Death
As a believer, when you look at death, learn to perceive it God's way. Death is an adversary of humankind and on behalf of all humankind, God defeated it through the death, burial, and resurrection of Yeshua. That means, as a human being dwelling upon this earth, your physical body will one day die,[52] however, Death

---
[52] Unless of course, you are alive when Yeshua returns to collect His Bride. In which case, at the sound of that trumpet, you will

has not the final word here! One day, God will raise your body from the dead and as the Apostle Paul said, "Death will be swallowed up in Victory"[53].

Spiritually, God made you alive in Messiah when He deposited the Holy Spirit within your being. This is a down payment of God's promise to do the whole job of redeeming your spirit, soul, and body!

In Summary

Believers, when born again, undergo a tremendous experience; however, they do not always feel that experience, even though it is very real. The Holy Spirit, by His own Power, translates the born-again person

---

meet Him in the air as this scripture declares: 1 Thessalonians 4:13-18 But I would not have you to be ignorant, brethren, concerning them which are asleep, that ye sorrow not, even as others which have no hope.: 14 For if we believe that Jesus died and rose again, even so them also which sleep in Jesus will God bring with him. 15 For this we say unto you by the word of the Lord, that we which are alive and remain unto the coming of the Lord shall not prevent them which are asleep. 16 For the Lord himself shall descend from heaven with a shout, with the voice of the archangel, and with the trump of God: and the dead in Christ shall rise first: 17 Then we which are alive and remain shall be caught up together with them in the clouds, to meet the Lord in the air: and so shall we ever be with the Lord. 18 Wherefore comfort one another with these words.

[53] 1 Corinthians 15:54 So when this corruptible shall have put on incorruption, and this mortal shall have put on immortality, then shall be brought to pass the saying that is written, Death is swallowed up in victory.

from the power of darkness, or the legal judicial deciding ability of that force, and places them within the Kingdom of God's dear Son, Yeshua. Believers must learn to operate from that new place. They must grasp the idea that the former spiritual laws applicable earlier in their past life, have now ended due to an edict from the Almighty, Who has both declared and then implemented their freedom. Thus, believers no longer live beneath the Law of Sin and Death but are freed from that law to live within the Law of the Spirit of Life. That law operates by faith and so, believers must understand it, believe it, and appropriate it.

Once again, it is a choice one must make to accept it and live within God's kingdom reality. If believers refuse to make the choice to learn, or once understood, to practice living by the Law of the Spirit of Life, their lack of truth leads them to a place where they live far below what God intended.

Beloved reader, it may be that you do not understand the laws of the kingdom of God, or perhaps, you think you never will. However, inside the born-again believer lives the Holy Spirit. He knows how all things, including how to help you access the way to live by the Law of the Spirit of Life. Therefore, submit your life to the Holy Spirit! Ask Him to open your mind to the truths you must grasp. Ask Him to teach you! Trust Him to lead and guide you. Then, remember, it is His delight to do so! God has a great destiny for you! In that destiny, you have a work that none other can do but you!

Accept God's help as a reality and thank Him, with the eye of faith for working it all out for you!

Remember, in Messiah, God made you to arise above the powers of darkness!

(COURSE 204 continued)

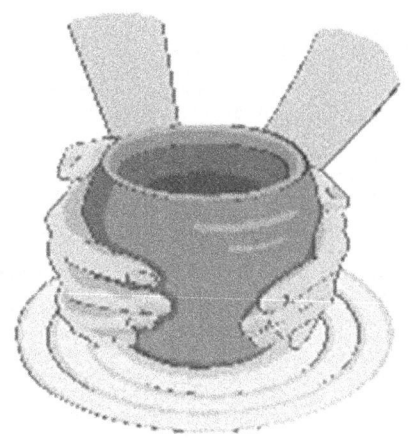

SECTION 3
MOLDED FOR GOD'S GLORY

 **Made for His Authority**

"For since by man came death, by man came also the resurrection of the dead. For as in Adam all die, even so in Christ shall all be made alive. But every man in his own order: Christ the first fruits; afterward, they that are Christ's at his coming. Then, cometh the end, when he shall have delivered up the kingdom to God, even the Father, when he shall have put down all rule and all authority and power".

1 *Corinthians 15:21-24*

Dear Reader, to get the best result from this chapter:
- Remember to see, as a reality, the believer's placement within the Kingdom of God's dear Son.
- *Remember too that when* God positioned the believer within the Kingdom of God, (His Dear Son), He implemented certain measures, the sum intentions of which bring change into a believer's life in order to give them a victorious life.
- *Remember the mention of o*ne such dynamic change as discussed in the last chapter: the *removal of every born-again believer from a life*

under the bondage of the Law of Sin and Death, to enjoy a new law, the Law of the Spirit of Life. To live under that the new law means accepting it as a fact and then, living in light of it. That requires a new mindset, the foundation of its shaping beginning with an agreement with God in this one fact: *believers are indeed translated from under the power, or legal judicial deciding ability of darkness.*

Even if you are not there yet, in your agreement with God's precepts, keep these above things in mind. Then, in this chapter, as you read of Yeshua's Ascension into Heaven and His position at God's right hand, you will better grasp the main point of the chapter, knowing why God incorporated Yeshua's exaltation and why and how, He applied it to your life.

Matthew[54], a disciple of Yeshua, closes His letter to Jewish believers with these words of Yeshua's spoken after His resurrection and shortly before His ascension:

---

[54] Matthew wrote this gospel to the Jewish brethren in Messiah. We know this because of the careful genealogy record within the gospel, but also, originally it was written in Hebrew.

Chapter 9   Made for His Authority

Matthew 28:18-20
> 18 And Jesus came and spoke unto them, saying, *All power* is given unto me in heaven and in earth. 19 Go you therefore, and teach all nations, baptizing them in the name of the Father, and of the Son, and of the Holy Ghost: 20 Teaching them to observe all things whatsoever I have commanded you: and, lo, I am with you always, [even] unto the end of the world. Amen.

God's gospel message must go to the ends of the earth and so, to facilitate the going forth of disciples to speak it, Yeshua declared He would accompany them. First, however, He tells them something He received: "all power in heaven and earth". That word "power", in Greek is <1849>⁵⁵ again the word εξουσια (ex-oo-see'-ah), which means legal judicial deciding ability.

Think about this:
- From Yeshua's resurrected and ascended place beside His Father, Yeshua declares that *He has "all legal judicial deciding ability in heaven and in earth"*. If Yeshua has "all", meaning the total and complete sum, then how much remains, in heaven and in earth, for someone else to have? The answer is none.

---

⁵⁵ Remember, this is the # Strong's Exhaustive Concordance uses to identify the Greek word < exousia> εξουσια

- If Yeshua has "all", meaning the total and complete sum, then how much of the "legal judicial deciding ability in heaven and in earth, does the power of darkness have? The answer again is none.

Yeshua has "all legal judicial deciding ability" in heaven and in earth. To say it another way, ***Yeshua is the only one who has the legal right to make all governmental (judgmental) decisions in heaven and in earth***. Those decisions come about by Him, for Him, through Him and in Him, as we will later see. Here, remember, the last chapter's message regarding this one scripture says:

Colossians 1:12-13
12 Giving thanks unto the Father, which hath made us meet to be partakers of the inheritance of the saints in light: 13 Who hath delivered us from the *power* <1849> *(legal, judicial, deciding ability)*[56] of darkness, and hath translated us into the kingdom of his dear Son:

Couple this statement with Matthew's statement[57] that Yeshua has the complete, total sum of all the legal, judicial, deciding ability in heaven and earth, we see

---

[56] This is the wording from the Greek meaning of the word as shown in the last chapter.
[57] Matthew 28:18-20

that the "power" of darkness does not have any *legal ability* to rule. Should it exercise any legal, judicial, deciding ability, it does so illegally!

When one considers further the remainder of Matthew 28 which gives commands to Yeshua's disciples to take the gospel message to the ends of the earth, this possession by Yeshua of "all" power in heaven and earth makes sense.

With that mind, let us look at Yeshua's legal, judicial, deciding ability. To put it into modern terms, let us look at Yeshua's Authority.

Yeshua's Authority
To reiterate Yeshua's words in Matthew 28:18-20, He possess the complete, whole, and total sum of legal, judicial, deciding ability in heaven and in earth. Thus, in light of that fact, believers must "go" and teach all nations. Many people, as they read that scripture conclude that Yeshua *delegated* His authority to believers in order for them to spread the gospel. In the Greek text in Matthew 28:18-20 **there is no indication of delegated authority.**

This statement puzzles some believers; however, a further look into New Testament concepts clarifies how *authority* works regarding believers. In order to grasp this, let us look at where Messiah sits today. We find

Paul's dissertation to the Ephesians gives us adequate information on the subject.

Ephesians 1:19-23
19 a) And what [is] the exceeding greatness of his *power* <1411[58]> to us-ward who believe, b) according to the working of his mighty *power,*<2904> 20 Which he wrought in Christ, when he raised him from the dead, and set [him] at his own right hand in the heavenly [places], 21 Far above all principality, and *power,* <1849> and might, and dominion, and every name that is named, not only in this world, but also in that which is to come: 22 And hath put all [things] under his feet, and gave him [to be] the head over all [things] to the church, 23 Which is his body, the fullness of him that fills all in all."

This verse is marked with numbers from Strong's Exhaustive Concordance to show which Greek word the Apostle used. It is as follows:
Vs 19 a):
- "His exceeding great *power*" <1411> uses the word δυναμις (doo'-nam-is) which implies great strength, might and a force like dynamite.

Vs 19 b):
- "According to the working of his mighty power" (verse 19) incorporates the word *power*

---
[58] Strong's Exhaustive Concordance number for this Greek word.

<2904> κρατος (krat'-os) which is a dominion and deed of power

These are different words with different meanings than in verse 21. These mean a dynamic, working power, which God exercised to place Yeshua in an exalted position. Let us define: *the position; the reason for it; what happens from that position and why God placed Messiah there.*

- **The Position**: "At His (the Father's) own right hand (verse 20)
- **The Reason:** To place Yeshua "far above all principality, power", *(εξουσια ex-oo-see'-ah, which is legal judicial deciding ability),* "might and dominion and every name that is named, not only in this world but in that which is to come". This agrees with Yeshua's own statement that Matthew recorded in that Yeshua "received *all authority*[59] in heaven and in earth".
- **From that Position:** All things are under His feet.
- **Why that Position:** He is the Head over all things to the church (the church which is His Body here on earth)

---

[59] This means ha satan has zero. Likewise, believers, on their own have zero, but when positioned in heavenly places, believers have access to one hundred per cent of His authority.

To recap, Yeshua sits at God's right Hand in a position superior to every government, spiritual or natural, upon the earth. He sits there as a King and makes decisions effective. There is no name like His Name, for it wields power into every realm of heaven and earth.

Yet, in the early part of verse 19, the Apostle Paul mentions these words, *"what is the exceeding greatness of his power to us ward who believe"*. This gives us a good clue to understand that what God did to Yeshua, He did for us. In other words, Yeshua's resurrection, ascension, and position at God's right Hand carried a purpose for all those who live in Him. He did it all with His own in mind. Paul's words in the next chapter explain this further.

Ephesians 2:4-10
> 4 But God, who is rich in mercy, for his great love wherewith he loved us, 5 Even when we were dead in sins, hath quickened[60] us together with Christ, *(by grace you are saved;)* 6 And hath raised us up together, and made us sit together in heavenly places in Christ Jesus: 7 That in the ages to come he might show the exceeding riches of his grace in his kindness toward us through Christ Jesus. 8 For *by grace are you saved through faith;* and that not of yourselves: it is the gift of God: 9 Not of works, lest

---

[60] Made us alive together with Messiah.

any man should boast. 10 For we are his workmanship, created in Christ Jesus unto good works, which God hath before ordained that we should walk in them.

When the Holy Spirit raised Yeshua and He took His place in heavenly places, bringing with Him that total judicial deciding ability, He immersed or placed all born again believers in Him. In other words, if you, dear reader are a believer, when Messiah sat in heavenly places, "you" sat there with Him. Due to this unique thing that God implemented, born again believers can, in fact *exercise Yeshua's authority*, *but not in a delegated fashion.* It cannot be delegated because, first, delegated authority is First Testament authority and therefore is not equal to what God planned for believers, since it was prior to the powerful works of the cross.[61]

Secondly, *delegated* authority, as seen under the First Covenant, *is removable.* Since Messiah's exaltation, He declared that He had "all authority", and beloved, that authority is forever secure in Him! He will never lose this! Remember, His dominion, by which we exercise due to our position in Messiah, happens because of His grace. That is unmerited favour on our part. Think about that for a moment! No wonder the Apostle Paul,

---

[61] If you have been taught about delegated authority in the New Covenant, please remain open minded as you read this chapter.

said twice in a few short verses, "by grace you are saved through faith". Once after declaring our position in Messiah, and another time prior to declaring believers as His workmanship, created for good works.

Regarding that workmanship of God, Paul relates as Ephesians 2:10 continues. God fashioned born again believers in Yeshua, for the sole purpose of good works, earlier ordained by God that we should walk in them. Whenever exercising His authority, no matter the works, it is using *Positional Authority*. In other words, the authority a believer exercises results, number 1 from Messiah's position in the heavenlies, and number 2, from the believer's position in Messiah.

This is a far greater form of authority. If one thinks about it, whenever it is properly, exercised, it is done in Messiah, for Messiah and through Messiah, and technically, by Messiah. The believer needs only to use it properly, within the context of bringing God's kingdom into situations and circumstances upon the earth.

Once we understand that authority never becomes ours, but always remains as the Messiah's, we centralize its use for things of God's kingdom and not for things of our own design. We utilize it for expanding the gospel, as Yeshua spoke of in Matthew 28:18-20.[62]

Understanding our position in Messiah we:

1. *Agree* with the release from the judicial deciding ability of darkness
2. *Agree* with the place of our translation into the Kingdom of God
3. *Agree* with the positional access to the judicial deciding ability of the Kingdom of God found in Yeshua

Beloved, remember to agree with God. Once you agree with God, you align yourself with God for a release of His Spirit in your life, to live out the Christian life with power and effectiveness upon this earth, and in the spiritual realms as well. You positioned yourself with adequate belief to function within the purpose for which God designed you.

Speaking of that purpose, if you think back to earlier chapters, humankind's purpose was to "watch over the

---

[62] Matthew 28:18 And Jesus came and spoke unto them, saying, All power is given unto me in heaven and in earth. 19 Go ye therefore, and teach all nations, baptizing them in the name of the Father, and of the Son, and of the Holy Ghost: 20 Teaching them to observe all things whatsoever I have commanded you: and, lo, I am with you always, [even] unto the end of the world. Amen.

doorways of the earth". Adam lost his authority to do so in the garden, when he sinned and unfortunately, at the same time lost that authority for all his seed.

Through Yeshua's obedience, however, God positioned humankind in Messiah for a position, which originates in heavenly places in Messiah. Believers in Messiah raised to sit in Messiah, now partake of God's Divine Nature which the Holy Spirit brings to fulfillment in the believer's life, as that believer yields to the Holy Spirit's lead.

Through the Holy Spirit, a believer, equipped and called by God, brings God's order into the earth. While God made Adam in His image and also equipped Adam to keep God's order, Adam failed. Believers, in Messiah, *by the exercise of their faith in Messiah*, can, succeed. Once more, the believer's choice makes the difference: *a choice, which is full of faith, a choice, which agrees with God.*

Chapter In In Summary
Yeshua's throne sits high above all principality, power, might and dominion, with a name far greater than any other name named in this world or the coming world. Due to the Holy Spirit's power and God's amazing gift, every believer sits in Messiah in His place of ascended victory. When believers recognize their position in Yeshua, they realize that no matter what they may encounter, Yeshua is greater and in Him, so are they!

His authority is all-inclusive, and believers, positioned in Him, exercise it to bring about God's will in every circumstance, situation, or event upon the earth.

This greatness and the expression of His authority does not depend upon the believer's own ideas or ability to rise above a thing. Rather, it *solely depends on Yeshua's already accomplished victories*. A believer's choice, once again, is to agree with God[63]. In that way, a believer aligns with God's revealed plans and purposes for their life, and in addition, position themselves to fulfill their purpose upon the earth. As believers do these things, they fulfill the command that says, **"the just shall live by faith"**!

---

[63] Remember, believers are made to align, which is another way of saying, made to agree.

Dear Reader:
- Do you see these marvellous truths, yet?
- Do you see what God designed for you, *after* your initial salvation or entrance into the Kingdom of God?
- Are you beginning to get excited about the characteristics of your new life in Messiah?
- Have you a glimpse of what "greatness" God implanted within you, His beautiful child?
- Have you thought of the joy of your position in Him, where you have access to Yeshua's "all authority"!

Beloved, take some time as ask the Holy Spirit to help you grasp these concepts from the Word of God. Understanding them brings life to you, and to all your being!

 Made for His Dominion

"Not everyone that saith unto me, Lord, Lord, shall enter into the kingdom of heaven; but he that doeth the will of my Father which is in heaven".

Matthew 7:21

Believers, utilizing an understanding of their position in Messiah in the heavenlies, situate themselves as instruments available to God in order to bring to pass His order and dominion upon the earth,[64] one incident at a time. Let us look at the validity of that statement. In order to do that, read once again God's commission to Adam.

Genesis 1:28

28 And God blessed them, and God said unto them, Be fruitful, and multiply, and replenish the earth, and subdue it: and have *dominion* over the fish of

---

[64] This is not a Kingdom now theory, which states God's kingdom, is here and now upon the earth. We will see later, the dominion given to humankind is for the purpose of bringing to pass on the earth the will of the Kingdom of God.

the sea, and over the fowl of the air, and over every living thing that moves upon the earth.

As recapped early in this book, the word dominion in Hebrew is "רדה" (raw-daw). The parent root (רד, resh & dalet) showed dominion over doorways, or entrance points, which symbolize events, situations and the like happening upon the earth. The child root, "הו"(heh), indicated victory.

Dominion then, in Hebrew pictograph language portrays a marvellous picture of *the authoritative tool of rulership or headship, over all doorways, which establishes a person as victorious.*

While Adam lost dominion, Yeshua retrieved and regained it. God positioned believers in Messiah, to exercise that *authoritative tool of rulership,* or in other words, to wield Yeshua's legal, judicial, deciding ability, with the purpose of bringing God's will to pass upon the earth. God's original intentions to see humankind live victoriously in his own life and in his task of watching over the doorways of the earth, is possible now in Messiah.

This is one more reason believers need to understand the Word of God. New Testament writers understood and recorded these principles, especially Paul, the Apostle. When he wrote Ephesians, recording the fact that God raised believers up together with Messiah, he did so with a dual reminder that we are saved by grace and not by works. No wonder! Only God could conceive of such a plan and then accomplish it.

It is A Matter of Rest
In an earlier chapter of this book, we looked at how God made humankind to rest. In that same chapter, additionally, we looked at the Hebrew word for "just" found in Habakkuk 2:4 which reads, "the *just* shall live by faith". In Hebrew, " צדיק " (tsad-deek), in the early pictograph language meant *"to rest in works that come from above"*.

Keeping these thoughts in mind, remember that believers in Yeshua enter their rest. Believers continue to live in that place of rest and from that place, live in the dominion made possible through Yeshua. This happens as believers:
1) Recognize their position in Messiah in heavenly places, and
2) Live out their Christian life from that position in Messiah.

Believers, who chose to accept the Word of God as truth, who embrace Salvation's principles, fully grasp the thought:
    a. they could not earn their salvation, and so, they rest in what God has done for them at the cross.

    b. Likewise, once believers comprehend their position in Messiah, they recognize the need to rest in the finished works or the cross from which they live out their Christian experience.

As the Apostle Paul stated, our place in Messiah happens through the power of the Holy Spirit.

Ephesians 2:5-6
> 5 Even when we were dead in sins, has quickened us together with Christ, (by grace ye are saved;) 6 And has raised us up together, and made us sit together in heavenly places in Christ Jesus:

To sum it up, believers, by the power of God, enjoy a baptism of the Spirit into the death, burial, resurrection, and ascension of Yeshua. As sitting denotes resting, believers must learn to accept the fact that God positioned them sit in heavenly places in Messiah, which means they live their Christian life from a place of spiritual rest!

Kings, when governing nations, sit upon designated thrones. From that position of authority, they issue commands. They do so, resting in the fact that they have the power on earth to do so. Similarly, judges, presiding over legal cases, rest in their appointed position to make legal decisions, which become law. Likewise, believers, whom God **_positioned in the heavenlies,_** were made to function from that place, a seated position in heaven, resting in all that Yeshua accomplished at the cross on behalf of mankind. From this position, they exercise the dominion, first given to Yeshua, and then to believers.

Remember this scripture from an earlier chapter?

Hebrews 11:6
> 6 But without faith it is impossible to please him: for he that comes to God must believe that he is, and that he is a rewarder of them that diligently seek him.

Faith shifts into its position from our place of rest as we understand God made all possible through Yeshua and the finished works of the cross. Afterall, as Yeshua walked the earth, He followed the finished works of His Father:

Revelation 13:7-8
> 7 And it was given unto him to make war with the saints, and to overcome them: and power was given him over all kindreds, and tongues, and nations. 8 And all that dwell upon the earth shall worship him, whose names are not written in the book of life of ***the Lamb slain from (before) the foundation of the world.***

In God's world, remember, Yeshua's work, which He accomplished on the cross, took place before the foundation of the world. Yeshua *believed and then rested* in *those finished works* of His Father, and thus produced for all humankind, the Salvation God prepared for us.

Upon entering through the door of Salvation, we cross over to a new life, one prepared for us earlier, in Yeshua. God equipped us to follow Yeshua's example, accepting by faith the works already done in every aspect of our lives. In short, we chose to walk by faith and in doing so, we have in front of us an open door to walk in Messiah's dominion. By faith and resting in those finished works, through the power of the Holy Spirit, we walk as Yeshua walked the earth, bringing God's will to pass in every situation.

God's plan for every believer and the position He gave us in Messiah makes it possible.

> Ephesians 2:8-10
> "8 For by grace are ye saved through faith; and that not of yourselves: [it is] the gift of God: 9 Not of works, lest any man should boast. 10 For we are his workmanship, created in Christ Jesus unto good works, which God hath before ordained that we should walk in them".

Verse 10 makes it clear! We are God's workmanship, created in Messiah to do good works, works that God already set in place that we should walk in them. Once this is understood and embraced by faith, the key to walking out the Christian life to its fullest is appropriated.

Speaking of keys, while upon the earth, Yeshua said this to His disciples:

Matthew 16:19
19 And I will give unto thee the keys of the kingdom of heaven: and whatsoever thou shall bind on earth shall be bound in heaven: and whatsoever thou shall loose on earth shall be loosed in heaven.

Since Matthew recorded this here, and again two chapters later, it is obvious that Yeshua thought this aspect of kingdom living important enough to repeat its mention.

In this phrase, "the *"keys of the kingdom"* we note its reference to disciples or believers of Yeshua, individually, and corporately. These keys of the kingdom of heaven, which Yeshua gave, speaks of authority from heaven released to His own. These keys, like everything else in the kingdom, operate by faith. When using those keys, keep in mind the tense and verse used in the original transcripts:

"And I give to you the keys of the kingdom of heaven: and whatsoever you shall bind on earth, has already been bound

in heaven: and whatsoever you shall loose on earth, has already been loosed in heaven".

Again, this is a reference to a finished work! Something done already, before you respond. This reiterates the resting factor, applying faith to the situation, realizing that it is done already. That is amazing! Even before the circumstances arose, and before you opened your mouth to declare, on behalf of heaven, Yeshua's legal, judicial deciding ability into a situation, it has already transpired. It has already taken place!

All things needed, in order for any situation to look like God's kingdom, ***stand in the wings***, waiting to enter, at the very moment you release the decision from heaven into that situation. The problem is, many believers *do not understand the "keys" which God entrusted them,* nor do they understand how, when, or where, to bind and loose things upon the earth. Consequently, situations rule believers and others too, instead of the other way around. Dominion, in those cases, believers fail to appropriate.

All within Messiah's Body, (which includes every born-again believer, young or old), who grasps this concept of the Keys of the Kingdom, can arise to a place where, individually and corporately, they represent and can affectively command God's intent or will upon the earth. When this is done, using compassion and mercy as it lies within God's heart for all humanity, the image of His character of God begins to align. Truth, then, can come into situations.

Believers have a responsibility to learn about their new life in Messiah, the character and nature of God of whom they must represent, and furthermore, walk in those principles. The more believers **learn** to understand the Word, **grasp** the ways, and means to walk in **dominion** upon the earth, **and then do it**, the more things on the earth have opportunity to come into alignment with God's will and kingdom.

In In Summary
In the opening of this chapter, it was said that *"Believers, utilizing an understanding of their position in Messiah in the heavenlies, situate themselves as instruments available to God in order to bring to pass His order and dominion upon the earth, one incident at a time."* That statement proves true, due to the power of God and the ability of the Holy Spirit to implement God's plans and purposes in the believer. All believers need do is learn, enter their rest, move in faith by cooperating with the Holy Spirit.

Every situation that a believer encounters in their life is "meat for God's kingdom". To put it in a more understandable way, a believer must learn to recognize and then grab hold of the opportunity in every situation, especially when things look as if they are going against the order of God, descending in a downward spiral. Remember, in every situation, a believer has a part to play, and this is to bring in God's dominion (His Will) into the situation.

Remember, dear believer, you are God's voice of authority on earth, exercising **Yeshua's legal judicial deciding ability into the situation.** Doing so, makes the problem ready for the mighty hand of God, the Holy Spirit, to align things with His kingdom.

You might think this is rather simplistic, in that life often seems complicated, however, we must remember, life, with all its human and spiritual factors, is *not complicated* for God. He knows every situation upon the earth and has already set the victory in place, on behalf of humanity. But it only *waits in the wings* for its entrance, an entrance you, dear reader, hasten, by obeying the Holy Spirit. The key to success here lies in the fact that believers need to move into a place of faith and take responsibility to see God's will declared into any given situation.

Recognizing that God seated believers in Messiah for dominion and stands behind His decision, should settle the mind to move ahead. Once the faith position activates, dear reader, and you take the action given to by the Holy Spirit, stay in that place of rest wherein the commands of heaven originated.

Walking in dominion, like every other aspect of kingdom living, begins with faith. Remember, God made you in His Image and made it possible, through Messiah, for a complete and total metamorphosis to return to that image. You can look like Yeshua in character, faith, and actions. Cooperate with Him and trust Him to do so!

Beloved, recognize
God made you for His dominion.
Then, walk in it.

 # Made for His Kingdom

"But seek ye first the kingdom of God, and his righteousness; and all these things shall be added unto you".

Matthew 6:33

Throughout this book, there has been much reference to the Kingdom of God. It is important that we understand, as much as possible about the Kingdom of God. While one book chapter cannot possibly contain all the teaching about God's kingdom, it can give a short overview through a small selection of Yeshua's comments and teachings on the Kingdom of God.

The Kingdom Of God Comes

Yeshua gave us a clear concept of the Kingdom of God *arriving* when He healed a blind and mute person.

> Matthew 12: 22
> 22 Then was brought unto him one possessed with a devil, blind, and dumb: and he healed him, insomuch that the blind and dumb both spake and saw.

The Pharisees took offence to Yeshua's ability to heal and accused Him of doing His mighty work from demonic power. As Yeshua explained the truth to the listening crowds, He refuted the accusation by the Pharisees and then added these words:

Matthew 12:28
> 28 But if I cast out devils by the Spirit of God, then the kingdom of God is come unto you.

With these words, Yeshua emphatically states the Kingdom of God comes, and when it does, the Spirit of God brings it. In the situation to which Matthew 12:28 refers, the blind and mute person received his sight as well as an ability to speak, as recorded in verse 22.

Regarding the kingdom of God coming, Matthew and Luke, in their gospels record the words of Yeshua, when He taught His disciples to pray:

Matthew 6:10
> 10 Thy kingdom come. Thy will be done in earth, as it is in heaven.

Once again, we see the Kingdom of God comes. Also, we see that its arrival intimately connects to the Will of God happening on the earth, in the same manner as His will takes place in heaven.

In the example shown in Matthew 12, the blind and mute person received his sight when the Kingdom of God came upon him. To look at differently, when the Kingdom of God touched the person's life, his life began to look like God's kingdom. That Kingdom operates in power, included restoration power to repair damaged bodies.

Mark 1:14-15
> 14 Now after that John was put in prison, Jesus came into Galilee, preaching the gospel of the kingdom of God, 15 And saying, The time is fulfilled, and the kingdom of God is at hand: repent ye, and believe the gospel.

Yeshua declared an intimate connection between the Kingdom of God and the gospel in that, when an unrepented (unsaved) person hears the gospel message, the Kingdom of God draws near to that person and is accessible to them. In Yeshua's words, "the Kingdom of God is at hand". This same idea, of the Kingdom coming, Yeshua conveyed when He instructed His disciples to go out before Him into all the cities where He would go.

Luke 10:8-9
> 8 And into whatsoever city ye enter, and they receive you, eat such things as are set before you: 9 And heal the sick that are therein, and say unto

them, The kingdom of God is come nigh unto you.

In this scripture, Yeshua associated healing with the Kingdom of God coming near.

In another reference to the Kingdom of God, we read:

> John 3:3-6
>> 3 Jesus answered and said unto him, Verily, verily, I say unto thee, ***Except a man be born again, he cannot see the kingdom of God.*** 4 Nicodemus saith unto him, How can a man be born when he is old? can he enter the second time into his mother's womb, and be born? 5 Jesus answered, Verily, verily, I say unto thee, ***Except a man be born of water and of the Spirit, he cannot enter into the kingdom of God.*** 6 That which is born of the flesh is flesh; and that which is born of the Spirit is spirit.

In this teaching of Yeshua's, we see the following:
- One cannot "see" the Kingdom of God unless they are born again.
- One cannot "enter" the Kingdom of God unless they are born of water and of the Spirit[65].
- The Kingdom is not a fleshly kingdom. It is one of Spirit. *(Born again people enter the Kingdom and*

---
[65] Means born-again.

are subject to its rules and laws. Fleshly laws and rules do not apply.)[66]

In Yeshua's time, the Pharisees asked about the Kingdom of God coming, however, they perceived it as a fleshly kingdom, one they could see and touch. In their minds, the Kingdom of God would overpower Rome, the then captors of the Jews. Once set free, the Jews intended to rule with power over all their enemies. Yeshua explained that the Kingdom of God was different than what they expected.

Luke 17:20-21
> 20 And when he was demanded of the Pharisees, when the kingdom of God should come, he answered them and said, The kingdom of God cometh not with observation: 21 Neither shall they say, Lo here! or, lo there! for, behold, the kingdom of God is within you.

God's kingdom arrival one does not perceive with human eyes, however, they can perceive its affect!

John 3:8
> "The wind bloweth where it listeth (wills), and thou

---

[66] The book entitled, *"Kingdom Keys for Kingdom Kids"*, authored by Jeanne Metcalf, covers the laws of the Kingdom of God to help believers know and walk in them. See Appendix for more details on how to order this book.

hearest the sound thereof, but canst not tell whence it cometh, and whither it goeth: so is every one that is born of the Spirit".

Those born of the Spirit are those who received Yeshua as Lord and Savour and are now baptized by the Holy Spirit into Yeshua, and function within the principles of the kingdom of God. You cannot tell these people belong to the kingdom of God with your eyes, for they do not look any different than another human being, however, as they move in Holy Spirit power, you see what happens as these bring in the will of God, such as Yeshua did when healing a deaf, blind, and mute person.

Regarding God's kingdom, no one can tell someone, get in your car and drive to such and such a place and there you will enter into that kingdom. It is not a kingdom of flesh! "The kingdom of God is within you". This statement helps us to understand that God's kingdom on earth is *an invisible kingdom*, with characteristics different from fleshly kingdoms. On that same theme, the Apostle Paul wrote:

> Romans 14:17
> 17 For the kingdom of God is not meat and drink; but righteousness, and peace, and joy in the Holy Ghost.

Fleshly kingdoms are temporal. One can touch those kingdoms. One can eat and drink in those kingdoms. God's kingdom, on the other hand, does not satisfy the flesh. God's kingdom concerns itself with eternal values, providing righteousness, peace, and joy in the Holy Spirit.

The following chart summarizes the foregoing scriptures regarding the Kingdom of God

Previous Scriptures on God's Kingdom[67]

Scripture	Kingdom Characteristic
Matthew 12:28	Spirit of God brings manifestation of the Kingdom
Matthew 6:10	The will of God associated with His Kingdom
Mark 1:14	Preached about by the gospel, and is near when messengers speak the gospel message
Luke 10:8	Yeshua's Disciples preach it. It is associated with healing.
John 3:3	Cannot be seen by the human eye, only when one is born again can they see it
John 3:6	The Kingdom cannot be entered unless one is born of water and of the Spirit (one is born of Spirit when they are born again)

---

[67] This is a partial summary of scriptures previously used.

Luke 17:20	It is not a physical kingdom one can watch approaching, but it is within
Romans 4:17	It is not meat and drink, (nothing physical from this world) but is righteousness, peace, and joy in the Holy Ghost

Basically, two themes are at work here.
1. For the unsaved, the Kingdom of God comes near when the gospel is preached
2. For the saved, the Kingdom of God lives within them (as the Holy Spirit comes and dwells in them)

In Summary:
- *The saved person*, the one who is born again, has the Holy Spirit dwelling within them, (they are born of God's Spirit). They experientially know the Kingdom of God, as, after their salvation, it moved within them. They operate from that Kingdom by the Holy Spirit, who dwells within.
- *The unsaved person* has yet to enjoy the benefits of God's kingdom within; however, they can experience it without, in ways such as hearing the gospel, or enjoying healing, etc. When the unsaved person repents of their sins and receives Salvation, then the Kingdom of God moves within.

This then is the basics of the Kingdom of God. Believers must understand that, wherever they go, the Kingdom of God goes too, and the Holy Spirit, who is within, accompanies them. Thus, following Yeshua's words makes great sense: "Behold, I am with you always, even to the end of the world" [68].

Thy Will Be Done

While the Kingdom of God is not flesh and blood, but rather is Spirit, some find it difficult to grasp. Admittedly, explaining it is not easy. Yeshua used several parables to explain its principles, but each time, Yeshua used something familiar to His listeners so they could grasp its meaning. Comparing God's kingdom to kingdoms on earth should help us to grasp it better.

Kingdoms on earth have one ruler, normally a King, but sometimes a Queen. In a complete Sovereignty, the monarch makes Laws, which govern the nation. At their disposal are armies who protect the nation from outside invasion and help with inside matters too. In addition, there are police personnel to enforce the laws, protecting the people within the nation, etc. These hired servants carry out the monarch's wishes throughout the land. In short, what the King wants, the King gets. Some kingdoms are cruel and unforgiving and rule with an iron hand, while some

---

[68] Matthew 28:2

maintain a kingdom, which ensures a good quality of life for all their citizens.

The kingdom of God, first, is a Kingdom which ensures a good quality of life for all its citizens. Within the Kingdom, there is on Ruler, God. God makes the Laws that govern His Kingdom. Yeshua summarized those laws by explaining their intent, when He taught the disciples to pray, "Thy Will be done". [69] These words are not a statement, but they constitute a command whereby one puts their foot down and says, "I will have nothing in my life today but God's will!" Thus, when one follows Yeshua's advice, they make that emphatic declaration, which, by faith, they expect to see materialize. The Spirit of God enters the scene and brings with Him whatsoever resolve the situation needed.

Far too often, we forget the part of the believer who prays, first at salvation to have the Kingdom of God move within, and secondly, who lives out their life, from their position, within God's kingdom. Remember, believers have use of the Keys of the Kingdom to see the Kingdom of God come into the lives of others. These Keys "bind" adversaries and "loose" them or remove them from their assignment. To understand that in modern terms, believers act as God's police personnel. By their faith and through their position in

---

[69] Matthew 6:10

the heavenlies, they enter situations and, with the tools God gave them, they arrest the bad entities, removing them from the scene, and then, peace comes in. With this kind of police work, there is no need for long, drawn out court cases, since God judged the adversary a long time ago, and so, with the command of "binding" and "loosing" given, the Holy Spirit enforces the commands and thus removes that adversary. The blessings follow with whatever the situation warranted.

Believers, in general then, have a sort of "cover all situation clause", and that is to command God's will be done on the earth. Understanding God's will, to many believers, becomes confusing at times, but as a rule of thumb, remember that God desires the best things for all people. If, dear reader, you find yourself stuck in dispensing God's will, ask this question: "How would Yeshua handle it, *if He were here instead of me?*" Think of Yeshua's life upon the earth, a summary of which Luke, the Apostle, mentioned in the book of Acts.

Acts 10:38
> 38 How God anointed Jesus of Nazareth with the Holy Ghost and with power: who went about doing good, and healing all that were oppressed of the devil; for God was with him.

If you are still stuck, simply state directly in the situation, in no uncertain terms, the Will of God comes in. Put your foot down, believing God will see to it that His will is done[70].

Dear reader, as you go from situation to situation throughout your life, remember, the Kingdom of God is within you. Remember also, your position in Yeshua in Heavenly Places. As a true, born-again believer you are God's authoritative voice on the earth to speak His commands as the Holy Spirit guides you. He is your life's coach on what to say, when and how to say it. He is the Comforter, the Teacher, and the One YeHoVaH sent to help you "get it".

In Summary:
God desires that His Kingdom touch every life and literally operate in every corner of the earth. He wishes that because He desires to provide the best care possible for all humankind. He wants the gift of eternal life to touch everyone. He wants the covenant relationship that He established for humankind to be each person's individual reality, so that each one can walk with Him and receive His blessings. His heart is full of love and compassion for all, and His Mercies are great. He desires to build up the broken, to repair the damaged, to secure beneath His Wings all those who are lost, wandering, or floundering in life, no matter

---

[70] A believer does not have to know the will of God to see it done.

the reason. He wants to establish them on a good foundation.

Believers, who know their God, will find bubbling up within them, these same desires for others. With a broadened understanding, they will embrace their full salvation, their position within Messiah, and their call to reach out to others. To see God's kingdom manifest in the lives of others, they will spend time with God to make intercession. It is a matter of learning the watchman's task, opening the mouth, and declaring, "Thy Kingdom come, Thy will be done, on earth as it is done in heaven above".

Beloved, understand that
God equipped you to walk by the power of His Spirit
for He made you for His Kingdom.

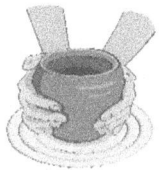 ## Made for His Purpose — 12

"Except the LORD build the house, they labour in vain that build it: except the LORD keep the city, the watchman wakes [but] in vain".

Psalm 127:1

In an earlier chapter, you read,
"Now that you know that God designed every human being to first "watch" over their life, and then "watch" over the happenings on the earth, you may ask, "how does one goes about watching?" In "Molded for the Miraculous", principles on how to watch are presented to help the reader understand a needed foundation for watching, and thus to fulfil their purpose of watching. The final Chapter returns to the theme of watching".

Thus, this chapter returns to the theme of watching, but first, a quick review of some major themes covered.

- God's creation of humankind gave them "dominion" to complete their task of watching over the doorways of the earth.
- Adam, through his choice, lost that "dominion", and opened a door to the Law of Sin and Death.
- Yeshua's work in His life, Death and Resurrection restored the "dominion" for all humankind who believe in Him.
- The Holy Spirit's implements that "dominion" in the life of a born-again believer, He baptizes them into Yeshua's death, burial, resurrection, and ascension into heavenly places.
- Believers in Messiah live under a new Law of the Spirit of Life which is a far greater Law than the Law of Sin and Death.
- God's calls all believers to know walk in that new Law of the Spirit of Life, and in doing so, walk in "Yeshua's dominion", to complete the all-important task of watching over the doorways of the earth.

Remember a believer's Divine Purpose upon the Earth is to "watch over the doorways of the earth", exercising "Messiah's dominion" to see the Will of God done in every situation. Now, let us look at watching, which, today, we call intercession. Keep in mind, this is only highlights of intercession.

Chapter 12 — Made for His Purpose

A watchman, as purposed by God and equipped by Him, stands guard over the doorways of the earth to bring in God's Will, in every place, and in every situation. The effectiveness of the watchman[71] depends upon many things, some of which include the faithfulness of the watchman (or intercessor), to learn the Word of God, listen to the Holy Spirit lead them in intercession, and take the time to complete any assignment given to them by the Spirit.

There is a passage of scripture, when clearly understood, shows a picture of how to watch over the doorways of the earth. We find that picture prophetically demonstrated in the life of Nehemiah.

Nehemiah 2:1-18

> *¹And it came to pass in the month Nisan, in the twentieth year of Artaxerxes the king, that wine was before him: and I took up the wine and gave it unto the king. Now I had not been beforetime sad in his presence. ²Wherefore the king said unto me, Why is thy countenance sad, seeing thou art not sick? this is nothing else but sorrow of heart. Then I was very sore afraid, ³And said unto the king, Let the king live forever: why*

---

[71] A good book devoted entirely to intercession and offered through Cegullah Publishing is called, Releasing the Impossible, subtitled, the Limitless power of Intercession. See Appendix for details.

should my countenance not be sad, when the city, the place of my fathers' sepulchers, lies waste, and the gates thereof are consumed with fire?

⁴Then the king said unto me, For what dost thou make request? So, I prayed to the God of heaven. ⁵And I said unto the king, If it pleases the king, and if thy servant has found favour in thy sight, that thou wouldest send me unto Judah, unto the city of my fathers' sepulchers, that I may build it. ⁶And the king said unto me, (the queen also sitting by him,) For how long shall thy journey be? and when wilt thou return? So, it pleased the king to send me; and I set him a time. ⁷Moreover I said unto the king, If it please the king, let letters be given me to the governors beyond the river, that they may convey me over till I come into Judah; ⁸And a letter unto Asaph the keeper of the king's forest, that he may give me timber to make beams for the gates of the palace which appertained to the house, and for the wall of the city, and for the house that I shall enter into. And the king granted me, according to the good hand of my God upon me.

⁹Then I came to the governors beyond the river and gave them the king's letters. Now the king had sent captains of the army and horsemen with me. ¹⁰When Sanballat the Horonite, and Tobiah the servant, the Ammonite, heard of it, it grieved them exceedingly that there was come a man to seek the welfare of the children of Israel. ¹¹So I came to Jerusalem and was there for three days.

¹²And I arose in the night, I, and some few men with me; neither told I any man what my God had put in my heart to do at Jerusalem: neither was there any beast with me, save the beast that I rode upon. ¹³And I went out by night by the gate of the valley, even before the dragon well, and to the dung port, and viewed the walls of Jerusalem, which were broken down, and the gates thereof were consumed with fire. ¹⁴Then I went on to the gate of the fountain, and to the king's pool: but there was no place for the beast that was under me to pass. ¹⁵Then went I up in the night by the brook, and viewed the wall, and turned back, and entered by the gate of the valley, and so returned. ¹⁶And the rulers knew not whither I went, or what I did; neither had I as yet told it to the Jews, nor to the priests, nor to the nobles, nor to the rulers, nor to the rest that did the work. ¹⁷Then said I unto them, Ye see the distress that we are in, how Jerusalem lies waste, and the gates thereof are burned with fire: come, and let us build up the wall of Jerusalem, that we be no more a reproach. ¹⁸Then I told them of the hand of my God, which was good upon me; as also the king's words that he had spoken unto me. And they said, Let us rise up and build. So, they strengthened their hands for this good work.

Gates And Walls in Nehemiah's Time

Nehemiah 2: 1-18 details an explanation of the reason Nehemiah, a cupbearer to King of Babylon, went to Jerusalem. Seventy some years earlier, King Nebuchadnezzar besieged Jerusalem and took its people away as captives to Babylon. Later, under the reign of another king, an edict came to rebuild Jerusalem. Returnees rebuilt the altar of sacrifice along with the temple, but the walls of the city of Jerusalem were broken down and the gates were missing, destroyed by fire during the siege.

In ancient times, very high and thick walls surrounded a city, and heavy gates protected entranceways into the city for the purpose of protection. Without this system of defence, a city with its inhabitants was very vulnerable. Any enemy could invade the city, rob its goods, kill, or enslave its inhabitant and burn the city. Walls and gates provided an effective "security system", and since the walls were high and thick, soldiers could walk the wall along the top ridge in order to recognize an invasion by enemy forces.

In addition, soldiers monitored the gates for possible trouble trying to sneak into the city past the security guards or watchman. If these soldiers were alert, threats were recognized and handled, thus averting trouble. In the case of an oncoming invasion, a warning sounded. This advance warning gave opportunity for the city to send out troops to thwart the attack and gave time to bring citizens without the city, to safety within the city's protective walls. This advance warning also gave time to dispatch messengers to an allied force to bring assistance.

When it came to protecting Jerusalem, from a spiritual perspective, while watchmen walked the walls, its walls really only *symbolized her* true defence: the Lord of Hosts. Under First Covenant Law, as long as God's people followed YeHoVaH and lived within His commandments, YeHoVaH promised His protective hand. If they sinned, they could ask YeHoVaH to forgive them and make atonement for their sin. Then, their walls of protection would remain strong. If, however, they did not forsake their sin but continued to walk in disobedience to God's Laws, refusing to repent and make atonement for their sin, YeHoVaH promised to remove His protection.

In the Bible we see that Nebuchadnezzar breached the walls of Jerusalem because Israel, after repeated warnings and calls to repentance from God refused to forsake their sin in forsaking YeHoVaH, His Laws and commands. Their spiritual protection lifted and thus, Nebuchadnezzar breached their walls and gates. After the siege and destruction of Jerusalem, she looked physically how she looked spiritually: *without walls and gates, vulnerable to enemy invasion.*

Looking at Jerusalem, *with a First Covenant mindset*, we see a *picture which, when understood shows the following things:*

1. Walking *within the laws of God* builds a protective wall around people's lives[72]. The gates represent choices and so, the task of every human being is to watch the "doorways" to *disallow sin's* entrance. *(Of course, no human being will have a complete set of fortified walls and gates because human beings sin, and also remember, they have inherent sin from Adam. For the sake of understanding, keep in mind that gates represent doorways or choices, and walls represent living within the laws of God.)*
2. If, like Cain and others, a person does not make choices in line with God's commandments, their gates open. Each time they do so, their point of protection weakens.
3. Eventually, with increasingly bad choices, **both door and walls collapse**, and that person becomes vulnerable. The adversary finds it easy to enter that person's life and bring destruction.

Yeshua sums the enemy's whims up in one statement:

John 10:10
> 10 *The thief cometh not, but for to steal, and to kill, and to destroy: I am come that they might have life, and that they might have it more abundantly.*

---

[72] This principle extends past lives and applies to families, cities, and nations.

When a person wants to *forsake their sin*, if they chose to do so they can receive God's provided solution, *which is Salvation*. This comes as they hear the message of Salvation, repent, and receive it. As discussed in an earlier chapter, once genuinely saved, the person has the Kingdom of God within. *Thus, in God's eyes, the walls and gates of the person's life are rebuilt spiritually,* and so now the saved person must learn to make better choices so with the help of the Holy Spirit, the walls and gates look, as they should.

A Clear Picture in Nehemiah 2:

Nehemiah had great concern for the returning Jews living in Jerusalem. They were vulnerable to attack and thus lived in unsafe conditions. Nehemiah, therefore, asked the reigning King of Persia[73], if he could return to Jerusalem to ensure its protection. With permission granted, Nehemiah returned to Jerusalem, and shortly after his arrival, he inspected the walls and gates. He then gave a report to the elders in the city as to his mission, and together, they made their plans and rebuilt the walls. That rebuilding project earned much opposition from the adversary in the land, but with determination, Nehemiah and his team fulfilled the edict to fortify the city, rebuilding its gates.

---

[73] Persia's roots go back to Babylon, the nation who conquered Jerusalem under King Nebuchadnezzar.

This action of Nehemiah and the elders rebuilding the protective walls of Jerusalem, gives a picture of believers *watching* over the lives of others. Once saved, the person now makes better choices in their own life, thus walking the wall of their own life. In other words, they keep an eye on their own life to ensure they live within the laws and commands of scripture.

Since God desires His Kingdom to expand, with a love for others from the Kingdom of God within, the believer learns to watch past their own life to watch over the lives of others, such as their family, friends, neighbours, church, province, nation, and nations of the world. This they do with the guidance of the Holy Spirit, through His power, using His wisdom and insight to see God's kingdom come into every situation.

We call this *"Walking the Wall"*. *This summarizes watching as it shows a daily system of defence that a watchman, or intercessor establishes through their prayer life or times of intercession. Through intercession believers build or maintain spiritual walls, preventing an enemy from conquering, pillaging, killing, or making slaves of those under an intercessor's spiritual watch.*

In short, believers watch over the doors of these lives, interceding for God's hand of protection, mercy, compassion, etc. for these people.

A BIBLICAL MINDSET:

Using Nehemiah, one can grasp the principle of "walking the wall. Through the prophet Isaiah, we discover God's heart in the matter.

> Isaiah 62:6-7
> *6I have set **watchmen upon thy walls**, O Jerusalem, which shall never hold their peace day nor night: ye that make mention of YeHoVaH, keep not silence, 7And give him no rest, till he establish, and till he make Jerusalem a praise in the earth.*

Here we see the task of a "watchman" over the city of Jerusalem. A watch person should never stop making mention of YeHoVaH. They are to intercede, giving Him no rest until He establishes and makes Jerusalem a praise in all the earth.

This scripture contains a watchman's focus, which is YeHoVaH; the watchman's duration, day and night, and the watchman's goal: *to see Jerusalem a praise in all the earth.* While this has a literal meaning, it also has **metaphorical meanings, one of which is souls saved and brought into the Kingdom of God.**

Spiritually, an intercessor can effect a situation where there is no influence in the natural. Through the power of intercession, an intercessor *watching* over a life[74] can

---

[74] Not only a life, but also the nations of the world.

monitor it and help to change the course of it. Of course, none of these things happen for the purposes of control. Every activity occurs solely to bring to pass the plans and purposes of the Lord[75]. In other words, to bring in the kingdom of God and see His will done!

Such interaction requires an intercessor developing a relationship with YeHoVaH to manifest these things. Thu, there is no better way to walk through the Christian life, or "walk the wall", then linked arm-in-arm with the Holy Spirit. He will help a believer to watch, teaching them how to walk the walls of their own life and those of others.

In Summary

God gave each believer the potential to be a powerful watchman, watching over the doors of the earth. Once they chose to partner with the Holy Spirit, learn to walk in the dominion of Messiah, they bring to the earth, *through intercession*, the will of God into every situation over which they watch. As a watchman, they understand their purpose is of supreme importance, and not at all a selfish one. As servants to God in Messiah, believers have great potential. They are one amazing gift of God to the earth!

---

[75] For a deeper understanding of watching, consider Watching. Waiting. Warning. See Appendix for details.

Chapter 12   Made for His Purpose

Knowing these things, dear reader, attain them with the help of Messiah. Learn to embrace, express, and fulfill your Christian life!

Remember, God positioned you to watch over the doors of the earth for His purpose: to see His kingdom come to pass in the lives of all who live upon the earth.

Beloved, live for God's your purpose!
Live your life with God to the fullest extent!
See His kingdom come and
His will done upon the earth!

CONCLUSION

In the beginning of this book, you read that there is an underlying purpose, which once embraced, forms a foundation on which to attain every aspect of spiritual and natural life, corporately and individually. The fulfillment of that unique purpose lies within your grasp as you develop *your relationship with God. Along with Him, you "watch" over the earth*, moving in a powerful spiritual manner, which affects the operation of the earth and all within it.

This commission to *"watch"*, which we outlined in an earlier chapter, we defined as everyone's basic purpose upon the earth, corporately and individually. We showed how Adam lost his dominion when he opened the door to sin. We saw how God, through Yeshua, restored that dominion. Once born again, believers, through the power of the Holy Spirit, can fulfill humankind's original purpose by becoming one of God's "watchers" over the earth.

Yes, as a born-again believer, you can watch over your own life and over those of others, as well as events that happen upon the earth.

In summary, due to the works of Yeshua and God's amazing ability to apply these victories to your life, you can learn to look, act, talk and walk like Yeshua, remembering that wherever you go, the Kingdom of God comes with you because you are part of that Kingdom, and that Kingdom lives within you.

As you watch over the earth, you do so with an understanding that God desires His Kingdom to touch every life and literally operate in every place on the earth. He wishes that to happen because He provides the best possible care for humankind, and to those ends, He wants the gift of Eternal Life to come to everyone. His heart is full of love and compassion for all, and His Mercies are great towards all humankind, whom He created. He desires to reach into people's lives, saved or unsaved, secure them beneath His protective wings and then, bind up the broken, and repair the damage done by the powers of darkness. The lost, wandering or floundering in life, for any reason, He longs to embrace and establish them upon a good foundation. He wants all humankind to enjoy the best things of life, here, as well as in eternity.

Believers, who know their God and experience is heart in this matter, find bubbling up within them, these same desires for others. With a broadened understanding received, they embrace their full salvation, including their position within Messiah, and their call to reach out to others, individually and corporately. To see God's kingdom manifest in the lives of others, they spend time with God as they make intercession. It is simply a matter of learning the watchman's task, opening the mouth, and declaring, "Thy Kingdom come, Thy will be done, on earth as it is done in heaven above". Next, they believe God responds!

Through the positional authority of Yeshua, which believers exercise, they remove, by binding and loosing, *whatever looks unlike the Kingdom of God*. Thus, that which resembles the power of Darkness, through intercession, they extract. Believers are God's police personnel, who arrest the spiritual enemies that seek to bring in the agenda and characteristics of the power of darkness.

Of course, the Holy Spirit implements the commands a believer gives, for as a true believer, with their eyes fixed on God's desires and passions, they function within God's heart, and on His behalf, intercede for others so they may be liberated from the influences of darkness, and be set free to attain their spiritual destiny.

Beloved, as you walk in this direction, please do not expect to arrive in one day. Like a marinated piece of food takes time to reach its good flavour, believers take time marinating in the Holy Spirit, dying to self, and pushing forward for the things of God's kingdom. Simply, commit yourself to God with your hearts' desire laid you in prayer. Then, walk in faith He has heard you and trust Him to teach you.

In conclusion, dear reader, if you are a believer, who desires to watch over the doors of the earth, then walk hand in hand with the Spirit of Dominion. This is part of your destiny! Now you know it is there; know it is attainable! Reach out to God for it and expect Him to answer you!

As you accept your responsibility to stand "watch" for God, you will find a robust life with the One Who redeemed you, and desires to walk by your side in an amazing capacity. Life will not bore you, dear reader, nor will you wander about trying to understand your purpose. You will find fulfillment in the One Who created you for His Glory.

To whatever degree you learn to watch over the earth, dear one, you will find it rewarding both in your life and in the way in which your life touches others. So,

Conclusion

beloved reader, learn, embrace, express, and fulfill your spiritual purpose on the earth! Make it a primary goal!

Remember God made you for His Glory, and as such you are

MOLDED FOR THE MIRACULOUS.

APPENDIX

A Name to Honour
יְהֹוָה
YeHoVaH[76]

If, today, someone asked you to tell them the name of your earthly father, without hesitation you would declare it. If, for some reason, you did not know the identity of your earthly father, you would say so. You might even give an explanation as to why that might be so. Thus said, if asked to relate the name of your heavenly Father, today, would you do so with ease, or would you draw a blank?

Most of Christendom, today, is ignorant *as to the name of the Father,* as well as the way to pronounce it. As the author of this book, I would like to join the ranks of those who wish to relate that name to the world. I believe that when we stand before the Father on the day that we give an account for our deeds in this body, it would be a good thing to know His Son, His Name!

---

[76] Based on information given by Michael Rood. Some from his work entitled, The Chronological Bible, and some from his YouTube videos. For more information see page 28 of the Chronological Bible.

About The Name

Did you know that the name of the Father appears at least 6,828 times in the Hebrew scriptures? Scribes recorded it with four specific Hebrew letters. They are as follows:

י	Pronounced yode, or yod
ה	Pronounced as hey
ו	Pronounced as Vav
ה	Pronounced as hey

For centuries, whenever the Jews come across these 4 letters they simply say, Adonai, or Ha Shem (meaning the name). They refuse to pronounce the name for several reasons, some of which we will look at momentarily. For now, let us look at whether their tradition affected Christianity. That we can easily do by looking at our Bibles to see the 4-letter name of the Father either written or substituted.

A quick look reveals that our KVJ Bibles, as well as many other versions, the 4-letter name presented to readers is a 4-letter English word, "YeHoVaH" [77].[78] Whether intentional or not, Christendom has followed the ancient tradition of the Jews.

---

[77] In some translations it is GOD.
[78] We also can shorten that name to YHVH (Yod, Heh, Vav, Heh)

An Ancient Tradition

In early second century times[79] Rabbis hid the pronunciation of the holy name of God. They did this by omitting the vowel pointings, which are necessary to make the name pronounceable. Hence, as they carefully wrote the scriptures, their omittance of the vowel pointings made the name unpronounceable. Historians believe there were two reasons why they did this:

i. According to Josephus, Rome, under the rule of Domitian, 81 to 96 CE, put to death anyone using the name of the Jewish or Christian God.
ii. Many believe that the Rabbis borrowed a tradition from pagans, whereby the name of their god was considered too holy to mention, so they called him "Ba-al" meaning Lord. The Jews adopted this practice and most still practice it today, even some Messianic Jews!

Tradition Continues

Bible translators followed their tradition for many reasons which are not presently known. It is possible, they forgot the pronunciation of the name, but more than likely, those who knew it, hid it.[80]. Whatever the reason, following this tradition caused Christians to continue in this tradition.

---

[79] Some scholars even dating further back.
[80] According to some, the Jews secretly knew the name.

Does that tradition offend the Heavenly Father?
If indeed its origin was Baal worship, then we can give a resounding Amen to the fact it offends God. In addition, as we look at scripture, see the Apostle, Peter, declaring that "whosoever shall call upon the name of YHVH[81] shall be saved.[82]" Clearly God desires that all, including the Gentiles, come to Him[83] for salvation.

An Historic Discovery

Today, some Hebrew scholars[84] have searched the world over for Hebrew manuscripts. In doing so, they found many Hebrew documents have the full name with vowels and therefore the pronunciation of the name. These scholars may different slightly in pronunciation, but nevertheless, they are making the name of YeHoVaH known today.

Our Saviour's Name Hidden in This Name

In looking at the Hebrew root of the name of the Father, pronounced *Yah-Ho **Vah'***, and looking at another scripture, we see something amazing about

---

[81] In a moment you will see that YHVH's Name is in our Saviour's Name.

[82] Joel 2:32; Acts 2:21

[83] If they call upon the name of YJVH, surely the Father will show them Yeshua! John 6:44

[84] Nehemiah Gordon, a Hebrew scholar, according to his testimony on his website continues to mention increasing numbers of incidents in manuscripts where the name of God with all vowel appointments appears.

our Saviour. In speaking of the Prophet, the one the Father would send and to whom all must listen and obey, YeHoVaH said that His name would be in the name of the Prophet.

Exodus 23:21 "Beware of him, and obey his voice, provoke him not; for he will not pardon your transgressions[85]: for my name [is] in him".

Our Saviour's name, as given by the angel was "Yehoshua", which means Salvation.

That name, with its Hebrew letters reads as:

י	**Pronounced yode or yod**
ה	**Pronounced hey**
ו	**Pronounced vav**
שׁ	Pronounced shin
ע	Pronounced ayin

The name of the Father (יְהֹוָה) is in the name of the Son! The first three letters of YeHoVaH show it! (Yod, Heh, Vav). Is it so amazing that the name of our Father is in the true name of the One YeHoVaH sent to redeem us!

---

[85] Please keep in mind that Yeshua bore the punishment for your sins. Your sins were not pardoned in the sense no punishment was paid. Yeshua atoned for them on your behalf!

Honour the Father's Name

Throughout this book, and all later books, as well as all accompanying audios and PowerPoints, it is the author's intention to widely use, proclaim and continually pronounce the name of the Father, as well as the name of Yeshua. Indeed, this breaks with tradition of many, however, thus far as we have shared the news of the Father's name and use Yeshua's birth name, reception has been excellent.

Name Challenge

Since, as of this reading, you are no longer ignorant of your heavenly Father's name, we invite you to join the unofficial network of proclaimers of the Father's name and shout it from the house tops. In doing so, you honour the Heavenly Father, our Savour Yeshua, and the Holy Spirit.

> *Romans 10:12-15*
>> *"12 For there is no difference between the Jew and the Greek: for the same Lord over all is rich unto all that call upon him. 13 For whosoever shall call upon the name of YeHoVaH shall be saved. 14 How then shall they call on him in whom they have not believed? and how shall they believe in him of whom they have not heard? and how shall they hear without a preacher? 15 And how shall they preach, except they be sent? as it is written, How beautiful are the feet of them that preach the gospel of peace and bring glad tidings of good things!"*

ABOUT THE KING JAMES VERSION

Scriptures quoted in this book *originate* from the KJV **public domain version** of the Bible, which means, no copyright exists on this version of the scripture. While some find this translation outdated, Jeanne, trained in the KJV still finds this version helpful, and uses it in all her books.

In using KJV, however, it is good to remember the following:
- Some words in the KJV have changed meaning over the centuries. To understand such words, look up the root word in its original language. In doing so, the meaning stands out. For example. KJV uses the word "conversation" however, in its original language it means moral character, or behaviour.
- When KJV spoke of humanity, they said, "humankind". When you read that word, or hear others speak about the scriptures using the term, "humankind", know it refers to all humankind, not a specific gender.

Due to tradition, the name of the Father, YeHoVaH appears as LORD, or at times as Jehovah. However, in all Jeanne's manuscripts, YeHoVaH or YHVH replaces the term LORD.

SALVATION'S MESSAGE

Yeshua, when walking on earth, said this:
John 3:14-18
> 14 And as Moses lifted up the serpent in the wilderness, even so must the Son of man be lifted up: 15 That whosoever believes in him should not perish but have eternal life. 16 For God so loved the world, that he gave his only begotten Son, that whosoever believes in him should not perish, but have everlasting life. 17 For God sent not his Son into the world to condemn the world; but that the world through him might be saved. 18 He that believes on him is not condemned: but he that believes not is condemned already, because he hath not believed in the name of the only begotten Son of God.

During the time of Moses, the children of Israel in the wilderness, rebelled against God, at which time poisonous serpents infiltrated the camp, killing many of the people. After seeking YeHoVaH for a solution to the problem, Moses followed God's instructions and made a bronze serpent fashioned and erected it on a pole in sight of the people. Whosoever wanted to live, must acknowledge their rebellion against YeHoVaH, and in doing so, look upon the erected pole and bronze serpent, to YeHoVaH, who gave them life in place of death, then they would live.

Yeshua said, just as Moses erected that bronze serpent in the wilderness, He would be lifted for all to see. This referred to the event, in the future, of Yeshua's crucifixion. During the time when the serpent hung on that pole, whosoever wanted to live and not die from the serpent's bite must acknowledge their rebellion, their sin against YeHoVaH.

Likewise, for those who wish to live eternally, they must look upon the cross of the crucified One, to Yeshua, who provided life for them. This was an act of love for all humankind, necessary because man is born from Adam, and thus is born with an inherent sin.

Secondly, man sins. The consequence of sin is death, and eternal death, wherein man will spend an eternity in darkness, away from YeHoVaH. Unfortunately, there is nothing humanly possible to reverse those consequences. Even if a person had made a genuine decision never to sin again, and for some reason they succeeded, all their good deeds and good living would not erase the penalty of eternal death.

There is only *one way* for Eternal Life to touch a person's life. That way, Yeshua explained to His listeners, comes *through the cross*.

Salvation comes by understanding these facts:

1. Yeshua, being the Son of God and the fulfilment of the scriptures, never sinned.
2. YeHoVaH, on behalf of every human being on the earth, chose to make Yeshua become as sin, in His Eyes, so that Yeshua might pay the penalty for sin, for all of humanity.
3. Yeshua paid that penalty. He died on the cross and was buried in a tomb.
4. Three days later, He rose again, appearing to His disciples, to show them the reality of His resurrection, to show them God vindicated Him and made Him both Lord and Messiah.
5. Yeshua could not stay in the tomb, because "death" comes to all who sin, but since Yeshua never sinned, therefore, death could not hold Him in the grave.
6. All those who come to Yeshua, to receive Him as their Saviour, receive liberty from sin and from its horrible consequence, eternal death.
7. They enter YeHoVaH's Kingdom and receive eternal life, as well as another gift: The Righteousness of Messiah. After salvation, when YeHoVaH looks upon a believer in Messiah, He sees Yeshua's perfect life and sees a redeemed believer, set aside for YeHoVaH. Since salvation has taken place in the believer, the Holy Spirit dwells within them.
8. All it takes to receive salvation from YeHoVaH is receiving His Messiah, fully repenting from

sinning against God[86]. YeHoVaH even gives the believer the faith to receive His gift of Salvation!

The Apostle Paul put it this way:

Ephesians 2:8
"For by grace are ye saved through faith; and that not of yourselves: it is the gift of God"

When you pray the following prayer, realize we present it here to get you started in your walk with YeHoVaH. Living out your salvation depends upon your commitment to follow through *from this point, onward*. From the moment of your commitment and onward, dear one, please seek YeHoVaH for His help in all things, including help to make your life align with truth, and in the end be a praise unto His name, forever!

SINNER'S PRAYER
& LIFETIME COMMITMENT

Heavenly, Father:
I acknowledge before You, YeHoVaH, that I am a sinner. I understand sin's punishment is a life without You, for all eternity. Thank You for sending Yeshua to the earth, as the Messiah. I understand

---

[86] *And against man. When a person steals, etc. they sin against both God and man. PLEASE NOTE: all references to "man", either by scripture or the author, refers to all humankind, not a specific gender.*

now that He died in my place, to take my punishment for my sins. I believe You raised Yeshua from the dead, and now that I accepted Him as my personal Saviour, my old life dies, and my new life begins. I humbly ask You to forgive me of my sins, and as of this moment, I receive Yeshua as my Saviour. I open my heart to receive the works of the cross that You provided for me through Yeshua, and with Your help, I will walk away from my sin, turning my back upon my own will and ways. I will now live my life seeking to obey Your Word and Your will. Help me to live, from this point onward, in a manner pleasing to You.

One more thing:
Remember, this gospel message comes with power. When you hear it, the Kingdom of God draws near to you. When you repent of your sins and receive Salvation, the Kingdom of God moves within. You cannot see it, feel it, or tell it from an outward observance. It is accepted, received, and lived out by faith! Seek out other believers in Messiah and may God bless you richly as you live your life, now, completely for Him!

So now, be sure and tell someone! Remember that a person believes with the heart unto righteousness and confesses with their mouth unto salvation, as spoken about in *Romans 10:10:*

10 For with the heart man believes unto righteousness; and with the mouth confession is made unto salvation

HEBREW WORD INDEX

ENGLISH WORD	PAGE
Adam	31
Deceitful	56
Desperately Wicked	57
Dominion	30
Faith	67
Ground	25
Heart	56
Intercessor	28
Just	59
Replenish	34
Subdue	34
Till	24

SCRIPTURE INDEX

1

1 Corinthians 15:21-24...131
1 Corinthians 15:31.... 92
1 Corinthians 15:54.. 126
1 Corinthians 2:16 75, 80
1 John 5:8..................... 79
1 Thessalonians 4:13-18. 126
1 Timothy 2:14............ 36

2

2 Corinthians 1:20...... 68
2 Corinthians 4:6...... 109
2 Peter 1:4................... 51

A

Acts 10:38.................. 167
Acts 18:3...................... 15
Acts 2:21..................... 195
Acts 26:15-18 105
Acts 26:18.................. 109
Acts 8:38-40 118

C

Colossians 1:1............ 118
Colossians 1:12-13 ... 134
Colossians 1:13...117, 122, 123
Colossians 1:9-13 116

D

Deuteronomy 30:19..111

E

Ephesians 1:19-23 136
Ephesians 2:10...........140
Ephesians 2:19-22 83
Ephesians 2:4-10 138
Ephesians 2:5-6 148
Ephesians 2:8.............202
Ephesians 2:8-10 150
Exodus 23:21 196
Exodus 33:14 47
Ezekiel 18:20..............112

G

Galatians 2:20..............93
Galatians 3:11..............53
Galatians 3:22-26 85
Galatians 3:6................65
Galatians 4:9................79
Galatians 5:1-7 86
Galatians 5:19-21 103
Galatians 5:22-25 122

Genesis 1:1 21
Genesis 1:26-28 ... 29, 100
Genesis 1:27 22
Genesis 1:28 .... 33, 145
Genesis 2:4-8 23
Genesis 3:17-20 48
Genesis 3:20-23 40
Genesis 3:23 .... 33, 38
Genesis 4:5-7 39
Genesis 4:7-8 41
Genesis 4:9 50

H

Habakkuk 2
4 62
Habakkuk 2:1 43
Habakkuk 2:4 ... 52, 58, 66, 147
Hebrews 10:38 53
Hebrews 11:1 65
Hebrews 11:6 .... 60, 149
Hebrews 3:11-18 52
Hebrews 4:1-2 60
Hebrews 4:3 59
Hebrews 8:8 b-10 71

I

Isaiah 35: 5 108
Isaiah 55:9 81
Isaiah 59:16 28

Isaiah 62:6-7 181
Isaiah 9:2 109

J

Jeremiah 17:9 55
Jeremiah 29:11 9
Joel 2:32 195
John 10: 7 52
John 10:10 178
John 3:14-18 199
John 3:3 163
John 3:3-6 160
John 3:5-8 51
John 3:6 163
John 3:8 161
John 6:4 195

L

Luke 10:8 163
Luke 10:8-9 159
Luke 17:20 164
Luke 17:20-21 161
Luke 24:45 109
Luke 4:18 104

M

Mark 1:14 163
Mark 1:14-15 159
Matthew 11:5 108
Matthew 12 159

Matthew 12: 22......... 157
Matthew 12:28.. 158, 163
Matthew 15:18........... 73
Matthew 16:19......... 151
Matthew 16:24........... 94
Matthew 16:24-25...... 92
Matthew 26:40-41...... 43
Matthew 28:18-2...... 134
Matthew 28:18-20 ... 133, 135, 141
Matthew 28:2............ 165
Matthew 6:10...158, 163, 166
Matthew 6:33............ 157
Matthew 7:21........... 145

N

Nehemiah 2: 1-18..... 175
Nehemiah 2:1-18...... 173

O

Obadiah 1:3............... 54

P

Proverbs 14:12.............58
Psalm 127:1................171
Psalm 130:6.................21
Psalm 146:8...............108
Psalms 107:8-20.........106

R

Revelation 13:7-8 61, 149
Romans 1:17................53
Romans 10:10:...........204
Romans 10:12-15.......197
Romans 10:17..............75
Romans 10:8 b) - 10....70
Romans 10:8-1.............74
Romans 12...................93
Romans 12:1-2.............89
Romans 14:17............162
Romans 3:27................99
Romans 4:17..............164
Romans 5:12.........37, 102
Romans 6:3-7.............120
Romans 8:11..............115
Romans 8:2........101, 115

OTHER BOOKS BY JEANNE METCALF

An Arsenal of Powerful Prayers [87]
Scriptural Prayers to Move Mountains
Arising Incense
A Believer's Priesthood
Above Artificial Intelligence
Finding God in a World of A.I.
Bible Study Basics
A Closer Look at God's Word
Candidate for A Miracle
Wisdom from the Miracles of Yeshua
Foundations of Revival
Biblical Evidence for Revival
His Reflection
What God longs to see in His People
Heaven's Greater Government
Behind the Scenes of Earth's Events
In The Name of Yehovah We Set Up Our Banners
Biblical use of Banners
It's All About Heaven
As Pictured in Scripture
Kingdom Keys for Kingdom Kids
Walking in Kingdom Power
Molded for the Miraculous
Why God made You
Our Secure Faith Heritage
Foundational Truths to an Unshakeable Walk with God

---

[87] This is a book of written prayers of assorted topics to help believers live a stronger, active faith. No workbook.

Releasing the Impossible
  The Limitless Power of Intercession
  Volume 1: Intercessions from the Author's Life
  Volume 2: Intercessions from Biblical Characters
  Workbook: Both Volumes compiled in Workbook.
Salvation Depicted in a Meal [88]
  An Hebraic Christian Guide to Passover
The Jeremiah Generation
  God's Response to Injustice
The Warrior Bride-
  God's Kingdom Advancing through Spiritual Warfare
Thy Kingdom Come
  Entering God's Rest in Prayer
Watching, Waiting, Warning
  Obeying Yeshua's Command to Watch & Pray
When Nations Rumble
  A Study of the Book of Amos
Worship in Spirit and In Truth [89]
  The Tabernacle of David - Past, Present & Future

---

[88] Haggadah (Guide) for a Christian Passover. No Workbook.
[89] Good sister book to "In the Name of YeHoVaH We Set Up Our Banners".

ABOUT JEANNE METCALF

Jeanne believes the Word of God opens a door to help every believer to know their God. That knowledge, once gleaned and retained, makes strong believers to help them stand in the real world in which we live, no matter their vocation.

With these convictions in mind, Jeanne, inspired and led by the Holy Spirit, began to write in the 1990's. Soon she developed inductive[90] style Bible Studies and self-published them for her students to use. With her major goal to equip the saints, she found that her sound teachings, presented with clarity and simplicity, made an impact. As long as her listeners put in their valuable time to study scripture and took Jeanne's advice to call upon the Holy Spirit to help them, they became powerful believers, transformed, prepared and ready to stand in their generation.

Today, former students who studied the Bible with Jeanne, as well current new students, testify as to the validity of Jeanne's writing and teaching gift. They love the clarity and simplicity of the Word as she presents it in a refreshing straightforward format.

---

[90] In the inductive Bible Study method, believers learn first by reading and studying the Word on their own, then they glean from the textbook. This study method often gives a better foundation to a believer's faith than sitting through lectures or speaker related teachings.

Thus, they encouraged Jeanne to make her books more widely available.

Therefore, Jeanne began Cegullah Publishing, and then a year later, opened Cegullah Apologetic Academy. The academy, in addition to presenting accredited, Bible Study material, invites all believers to either read or study the Word of God, and thereby, be strong in YeHoVaH and the strength of His might.

A greater availability of Jeanne's works *(as well as other authors which Cegullah Publishing looks forward to publishing in the future),* opens doors for more people to know their God and do exploits!

*"**But the people that know their God shall be strong and do exploits**".* Daniel 11:32 b

***

CEGULLAH PUBLISHING & APOLOGETICS ACADEMY.

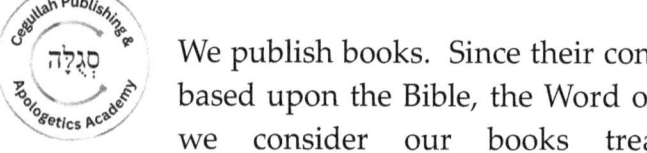

We publish books. Since their content is based upon the Bible, the Word of God, we consider our books treasures. Through these available treasures, we give opportunities for our reading audience to explore pertinent topics which steady, reaffirm, and help them to walk out their life in victory.

Our Vision
- To supply Christian, Bible-based materials to help readers study God's Word

Our Focus
- To help our readers to know *what they believe and why.*

Our Mission
- To provide Biblical, educational tools to help readers to know their God and connect with Him.

Our Publishing Motto:
- *Publishing the treasures of modern-day scribes.*

Our Academy Motto:
- *Earnestly contend for the faith once given to the saints.*

CONTACT INFORMATION
www.cegullahpublishing.ca

www.ingramcontent.com/pod-product-compliance
Lightning Source LLC
Chambersburg PA
CBHW060513090426
42735CB00011B/2197